FINDING YOUR SOUL MATE

MICHAEL

fINDING
YOUR SOUL MATE

SAMUEL WEISER, INC.

York Beach, Maine

First published in 1992 by
Samuel Weiser, Inc.
Box 612
York Beach, Maine 03910

99 98 97 96 95 94 93
10 9 8 7 6 5 4 3

Library of Congress Cataloging-in-Publication Data

Michael
    Finding your soul mate / Michael.
        p.   cm.
    1. Interpersonal relations--Psychic aspects.   2. Inter-
personal attraction--Miscellanea.   I. Title.
BF1045.I58M53   1992
131--dc20   92-20660
                                                  CIP
ISBN 0-87728-765-1
BJ

Cover illustration copyright © 1992 Richard Stodart. Used by
kind permission.

Typeset in 11 point Bembo

Printed in the United States of America

The paper used in this publication meets the minimum require-
ments of the American National Standard for Permanence of Paper
for Printed Library Materials Z39.48-1984.

Dedicated to all soul mates in our magnetic
and electric universe! And to my Maria.

Twin Buds Of Life

I

A single note swells,
  a half-tone sounds...
The echo flits through space
  and now returns
  ever marked in time.

II

Two lives flower,
  two buds touch hearts,
    A dual stream of pure love
    ascends and merges
    with the shining point
    of fire overhead.

Twin points fuse and flare
    into greater brilliance.
  A clear white light flashes forth
    to light the dual way.

A golden path merges...
  mysteriously, it becomes us.
Two individual selves fade out
  to find themselves doubly whole.
Single, yet both wed
  at another, higher, more
  revealing plateau.

Contents

Preface

What is most important to me is not how many books I sell and how much money I make, but rather making the most valuable gift of knowledge I can to you, the reader, in exchange for the valuable money and time you give to purchasing and reading this volume. This demonstrates the law of balance between us and makes the interchange one of equal value.

Why an updated, revised, and enlarged edition?

Several factors have influenced this decision. Most important is that I now have a grasp of "The Science Of True Mates" that was not consciously known to me when the first edition of *Finding Your Soul Mate* was published. Another influence is the great public contribution to this subject by my friend Jess Stearn in his wonderful best-selling book, *Soulmates*, published by Bantam Books.[1]

For over fifteen years, my own book, *Finding Your Soul Mate*, has been a best-seller in almost every bookstore, church, or meta-physical outlet that carried it. To date, this title has already sold 70,000 copies, without the aid of any major bookstore chain or book distributor. Through most of these past fifteen years *Finding Your Soul Mate* has been the only major published work that has addressed this timely subject of soul mates. This seems astounding when you consider this compelling subject is almost constantly on the minds of millions and millions of single or wedded individuals. Fortunately, after reading and using the easy how-to-do-it techniques revealed in my book, thousands upon thousands of thankful and joyous women and men have focused on and drawn their very own special "loved ones" into their lives.

---

[1] Jess Stearn, *Soulmates* (New York: Bantam, 1985).

To date, over these years, scores of enterprising teachers and lecturers have borrowed the format outlined in my book to teach classes and workshops using these proven techniques of bringing soul mates into their lives. All these teachers have my warm encouragement to spread this wonderful revelation about love relationships that are so special. Everyone on earth deserves a grand and divine love life, which comes when love is known and re-given! I know I deserve it, and I certainly hope you know you do as well! If not, it is time to change your self-image!

I give silent thanks as more and more orthodox bookstores buy and sell more copies of *Finding Your Soul Mate*. I give silent thanks as growing ranks of awakened or enlightened teachers relate "The Science of True Mates" to their students. Gradually, over the past two decades, I have developed the concept of soul mates and seen it become not only accepted, but very popular.

Again, what is so astounding is that over the years, despite the fact that major book publishers were either blind or purely ignorant to the need of a good book on this subject, I continued to sell and reprint this volume. I simply sold copies of *Finding Your Soul Mate* at my lectures or workshops, through mail order, and through a select, but few quality bookstores across the country. This needed book sold nationwide mostly by word-of-mouth as one reader told another about it. I hope you will do the same.

Shortly after Jess Stearn compiled and released his marvelous book on this subject, I decided to follow through on my own plans to revise and update this book. It has changed considerably. The science is now exact. I have also grown and evolved myself through these shining years!

I do indeed give honor and thanks to Jess Stearn in several ways. His book, *Soulmates*, highlights scores of soul mate relationships between prominent figures on the national stage, people like Shirley MacLaine, Richard Burton, Elizabeth Taylor, Susan Strasberg, Jeff and J.Z. Knight, Patrick and Gael Flanagan, and many others. I even had the honor and pleasure of performing a marriage ceremony for Patrick and Gael.

Jess speaks about Dick Sutphen and his beloved soul mate, Tara, who I also count as my friends. Needless to say, Jess has added a quantum of credibility to this subject, even predicting, while gathering information from me for his own book, that his book would help my own book to sell more copies, a prediction now well on its way to fulfillment!

In one last tribute to Jess, he unknowingly inspired me to move forward and revise this edition. He did it quite innocently. Jess was gathering information for his book and after a long afternoon interview with me at the Hilton Hotel in San Diego, Jess wrote that I taught that "the individual has to rigidly program himself, or herself, physically, mentally, and visually."

I was shocked when I read this! I realized that even though my techniques had been highly successful for many readers of my book, to a finely tuned and scholarly researcher like Jess Stearn they appeared "rigid."

My image of myself up until then was that my thoughts and ideas were extremely open and flexible. My pride took a big fall and I needed it. I was immediately jolted into an awareness that insightful Jess was probably right. I was instantly moved to re-evaluate my mode of thinking and teaching, for if it was "rigid," I had better fix it. Perhaps I needed to know and express myself in a more flowing and open way. My knowledge, thoughts, and feelings have evolved gradually over the years and I now see this science in a whole new light. In that humble vein, I will move on to present this beloved subject of soul-mating to you in the most plain and flexible manner possible. I truly want to gift you with the inspiration to know and bring your own soul mate into your life. Feel free to write to me in care of this publisher. I love and bless all of you.

———Michael

Introduction

In this book, I present the concept of finding your soul mate at two levels. To begin, I relate soul-mating to the Magnetic Universe, that half of all creation behind the moving visible world of effect. This is the silent world of cause and the reason why all things, all forms of life, are eternally connected to all other things and all other forms of life. It is the scientific *why* soul mates are magnetically drawn to each other, why "like seeks like" quite naturally. Scientifically, it is the undivided universe without end or beginning, which is only possible because we also live in the Electric Universe.

Secondly, I discuss how soul mates manifest in the Electric Universe through which we relate to visible nature, to our three-dimensional world of duality. This world is composed of a genuine sexual female or male polarity, centered within each tiny or huge form—whether mineral, vegetable, animal, or human. Everything in this seemingly formed universe, whether seen or unseen, is purely electrical in nature. There are no exceptions. All sexual actions and reactions are simply electric waves seemingly in motion, creating a platform or stage for the drama of infinite forms of life to unfold. The fully correct scientific term describing this extension of the One Light is the divided and multiplied universe, since the division and multiplication are needed to keep an absolute zero universe from which all ideas and thoughts in the form of light are extended into forever.

Ellen Chubbelle Pietsch

1

The Gift of Love

There is always an inner awareness that a soul mate exists.
So then begins the ecstatic, divine search.

The greatest gift any one can give another is the priceless gift of true love! That gift has nothing to do with physical objects, "making love," or possessions. All those fast-fading or seemingly lasting material acts or forms soon disappear from sight and human memory.

What lasts forever, on the other hand, indelibly recorded forever as a seed in the soul, is the divine loving gift of self to another self. This means simply giving your attention and time, your physical, mental feeling and presence when needed to loved ones, family, friends, co-workers, neighbors or complete strangers.

What you give of yourself or of your substance you never lose! While what you hold tightly to yourself, time will inevitably take sorrowfully away from you. In that light then, a gift of a much needed, or simply appreciated smile, a nod of greeting, a pat on the back, a word of encouragement, or physical "things" like food, shelter, or a glorious bouquet of flowers *when given with unconditional love*, expecting nothing in return, is a truly loving gift, because your living essence is in it! It blesses, uplifts and balances all concerned.

Not only is it wonderfully divine to "gift" this truly pure and unconditioned love to others, but you must also learn to "gift it" freely to yourself. The same immutable law applies here. You always get what you give! When you gift yourself with love it means that you now have overflow love to re-give to others. Self-love comes from self-respect. Give honor, respect and acts of high character to others and you immediately begin to find and love these divine qualities in yourself. Once these qualities are your major style of expression, you will automatically gift others with these grand essences simply through your brightly lighted presence with them.

I know you are reading this book because you are hopefully anxious to be gifted with a divinely grand love, which you can then, of course, re-give divinely to your most beloved mate. May many of these ideas gifted in love to you in this volume "catch fire" in your soul and inspire you with the intense desire needed to find your own wonderfully equal and balancing mate. May your own life and being *become* a gift of love.

2

I Found a Mate

*Suddenly, somewhere in this world, he or she will appear! What
joy, what peace, what soul-sounding, heart-pounding new love!*

If you have truly decided that you want to manifest a loving soul mate
into your life, and are willing to take the simple A-B-C steps to make
it so, I will gladly guide you toward your known desire. On the other
side of the fence, your soul mate is just as anxious to be looking
lovingly into your eyes, to touch your physical hand, and to share
beautiful dreams with you, as you are in doing all these longed-for
things with him or her! I personally know what it feels like to
experience the divine feelings, thoughts, and sensuous interactions
with the "girl of my dreams." I love and am ecstatically married to
such a mate this day.

Thousands of women and men who have read earlier editions
of *Finding Your Soul Mate* have also found their beloved soul mates
by following the simple proven how-to-do-it instructions relayed to
you in the following chapters. I happily found my soul mate and you
can do it, too. Enjoy this journey now as I take you with me for a
pleasant walk back through time.

From the beginning, certain wonderful sensuous dreams bridged
the distant space between this unusual mate and myself. Even the

word "dream" was a vital connecting link that suddenly and dramatically merged the two of us together. I am saying that from time to time this attractive female and I met unconsciously together in dreams during our regular sleeping hours. These mysterious, marvelously uplifting dreams began about two years before we physically met.

Thinking back, I have no recall precisely when we first began to meet in dreams together. Over a period of months, I gradually realized I was dreaming constantly about the same beautiful girl. There was something vaguely familiar about her. No matter how hard I tried, I could not figure what that familiarity was all about. I finally seized and fixed on the reasonable idea that I was simply dreaming about my lost love of the past, named Bonnie. It finally dawned on me that there were many uniquely different aspects about this dream girl. The tone, or aura, was different. It could not be Bonnie, after all. Known or unknown, I nevertheless continued to experience many more sensuous and love-filled dreams with my sweet dream lover.

Some of these soul mate dreams were ordinary enough, except that after each one I always felt wonderfully uplifted when I awoke. At other times, our courtship in the dreams was exquisite. The dreams were romantic, passionate, and like no other dreams I could remember! In the morning, I would awaken with such greatly enhanced zest and vitality that the feeling would last through the entire day. There were times when the warm soothing aura of my ecstatic dream encounters would physically permeate and linger in my conscious mind for days afterward.

It suddenly registered like a bolt of light one day how unique and fantastic it was for me to dream about this alluring girl. Lingering memories of the loving moments we had enjoyed together in dreams would often replay themselves through the new day.

All these dreams were spontaneous until one inspired evening I decided to conduct a metaphysical experiment. I had just finished reading an inspiring book on self-suggestion. Before falling to sleep, following the suggestions in the book, I gave myself the self-program to dream purposefully about my dream girl that evening. I calculated that if self-suggestion really worked, then at will I could enjoyably increase the frequency of nightly love sessions with my dream lover. Just before falling asleep, I gave myself the following worded suggestion with passionate feeling: "Tonight, I am going to dream about my dream girl again!"

Nothing happened the first night, or the second. Persistence is one of my intentionally developed characteristics, so I kept right on making the exact same worded suggestion each evening just before drifting away into sleep. *Bingo!* On the fourth consecutive night it worked! At some time before dawn I found myself plunged deep into a long and vivid dream romance with her. I congratulated myself the first thing upon awakening in the morning and resolved to do it again that evening. The day passed filled with sweet memories of my dream. When bedtime arrived, I gave myself the same memorized suggestion, knowing it would work, and it did. I knew from that moment on, I had found the magic key to midnight romance at will! Sure enough, by midnight or soon thereafter, we were both lovingly entwined in each other's arms.

Several times a week I would successfully "program" myself to "dream a little dream" about my mystery girl. It was really a fantastic arrangement, as far as I was concerned. My dream lover was virtually at my "beck and call." Over the next few months, I became more and more proficient in evoking her into my dreams. Upon demand, my dreams were an assured source of joy and sensual fulfillment. Looking back now, I still recall how much I then looked forward to going to sleep and dreaming during that phase of my existence. To this day, many years later, I still enjoy going to sleep and adventuring in the dream world, though not with a dream lover, since I am physically with my own true mate now.

Little did I know then that my dream mate would literally materialize at arm's length from me within half a year. It was almost exactly six months to the day when I actually met Pam. This is what helped lead me to her. My older brother, Richard, had suddenly died of a heart attack. A few days after his death, I managed to use suggestion to meet him in a dream. The following dream was a key connection to my dream mate. It is even more extraordinary than all my earlier dreams because I deliberately suggested and produced an actual face-to-face meeting of my soul and spirit, with his soul and spirit, in a most vivid, most colorful, and satisfying dream that evening.

My family had tearfully buried the body of my brother in Michigan, well over a thousand miles away. I lived in Virginia Beach, and had not attended the funeral—not because of the distance—but because I already knew, *there is no death.* That night before sleep, my mind moved to the sad realization that Richard and I had not seen or talked to each other for several years. His very unexpected death came as a terrible shock to me, as well as to my two brothers, two sisters, my mother, his wife and family, and a huge throng of friends. I felt genuinely sad that he left our three-dimensional earth plane, but I knew he was also quite fully alive. He had chosen and found freedom for himself—freedom from the limitations of the physical body—by simply changing residence from his mortal to his immortal body. My very dear brother Richard had led a truly model life on earth. He had been greatly loved and respected by all who knew him. He had character, charisma, and personality. We had all been fortunate to have known him. My one regret was that he died before I told him how much I loved and respected him, that he had been a model elder brother for me.

With these thoughts swirling and brimming over in my mind, I spontaneously decided to make use of my dream suggestion technique, but with a unique twist. This time, I suggested that my consciousness would reach up out of my physical body, by way of dreams, to the plane of soul and spirit, where I knew my brother Richard now dwelled. Even the little self-training I had in the "mysteries" had taught me that the real essence of my brother Richard was just as alive on the inner magnetic planes of the soul, as it had been while he wore his physical robe in our three-dimensional world. *The "kingdom of heaven is within!"*

With great resolve, I focused all the power I could muster into building up that strong feeling desire. At the same moment, I consciously gave myself the suggestion that, through a dream, I would rise up and meet Richard on the inner plane of the soul that night. I repeated this self-command over and over in my mind until I exhaustedly fell into a deep, deep sleep.

At some time during the night it happened. A vivid dream began to coalesce and take form as a registration in my physical brain consciousness. The memory of it remained indelibly impressed on my mind, during the experience, and upon awakening.

In the dream, my dream girl and I were sitting side-by-side as passengers in the back seat of a large, long hearse-like black car. A strangely familiar couple sat in the front seat before us. The man in the front, who was driving the car, carefully approached what appeared to be an open gate ahead of us, and we all knew this was our destination. He came to a stop, turned the car around and slowly backed it into the open gate. He stopped the car at the halfway point exactly, and parked so that the front part of the car, where the driver and his companion sat, extended outside the gate. The back half of the vehicle, where my dream girl and I sat, now extended inside the gate. My dream girl and I were now far enough inside of the gate so we could easily open up the back doors of the car and get out, or should I say, "get in!" There was a perfectly reasonable explanation why the vehicle had to remain parked halfway through the gate, beside the fact it then could not close on us.

At that time I gave no thought to it, since dreams always have their own reasoning. A few days later, as I pondered this dream, I realized the car was literally a symbol of our physical and spiritual bodies bridged between two worlds. Obviously, the familiar couple in the front were simply our own three-dimensional forms, still connected to our dreaming earth bodies and minds.

In my dream, with rising joy, I knew I had made my greatly desired transition into the world of soul and spirit. I was actually visiting Richard. I saw a rapidly approaching light and also knew the light was Richard. I left my dream girl standing by the gate and ran rapidly toward the approaching light. The light transformed into the familiar physical human form of my dear brother, who extended open arms to me! We hugged and pounded each other gleefully! Oh, what a joyful reunion! We spoke of the many "earth years" that had gone by since we had last seen each other. We talked and talked, sharing many wonderful memories together. I told Richard I loved him greatly and how much I appreciated what a model brother he had been. I told him that all through my teens I wanted to grow up to be just like him! Everything that needed to be said was said!

All at once, I realized our time together had come to an end. So did Richard. But just before we embraced for a final goodbye, Richard miraculously "manifested" an assorted bunch of dried fruits before my eyes. He handed them to me with a smile.

"Now, about your health, Michael," he said, "be sure you start eating more dried fruit. And your system should have more vitamin K. Soak some dried apples in water and drink it as a tonic. It will help you build up and enjoy the health you need and want!"

While in the dream, I overlooked the sudden manifestation of the fruit miracle. However, I was duly impressed by such brotherly concern for my health, as well as feeling pleased by the unexpected, though highly interesting information. I thanked Richard for it and gave him a long final goodbye hug. I could feel his love surging through me at the same time. I turned and dashed hurriedly back to the waiting car at the gate, and to my dream girl, who was patiently waiting there for me. A deep sense of urgency inside my being told me that time was running out rapidly. I must hurry!

My dream girl also felt this sense of great urgency, and quickly opened the back door as I approached, and we slid into the back seat together. Instantly, the familiar couple, also waiting silently and patiently in the front seat, moved into action. The driver put the sleek long car into low gear and gently eased out of the gate.

"Click!"

As the car cleared the gate, it suddenly and dramatically changed form. It was now a huge, wide and long "two seater" surfboard airship, soaring through the softly lighted dawn sky like a magic carpet. The couple in the front seat had totally disappeared from sight. Only my dream girl and I sat, now perched precariously on the high flying surfboard. I noticed that my dream girl sat directly mid-center and was deftly handling the controls of our high riding craft. I sat slightly off to her right side, thoroughly enjoying our ride together on the almost rocket-shaped flying surfboard. It was a thrilling sight! Millions of bright stars twinkled overhead. Below, thousands of feet underneath us, huge, slowly surging blue waves with frothy white caps picked up sudden speed and dashed wildly up the golden shore, then rolled back slowly, merging once more into the deep. The wide sandy beach extended to the horizon before us. It felt like we were flying high above the outskirts of Virginia Beach, headed almost due north. We both felt an exhilarated joy as the balmy warm air whistled and rushed wildly past our faces. I glanced toward my dream girl and wondered if she was capable of handling the mighty wind power. Could she steer our swiftly flying vehicle safely? I also felt, because I was sitting a little off-center, I might be throwing our flimsy airship off balance. There was a fleeing moment of worry that we might fall. My sudden doubt was instantly replaced with a deep realization that she was an excellent driver. There was no need for me to worry in the slightest about her ability to control the balance and movement of our craft. Simultaneously, I felt an irresistible yearning to move close, to snuggle near her and bask in the sheer joy of her physical presence. With the speed of thought, the two of us were rapturously intertwined snugly together. We soared on freely through the air toward some mutual expectant destination. We were both aglow with a deep "inner love" and the exquisite pleasure of each other's company.

On that seemingly eternal love-filled note, I awakened from this marvelous dream. I stayed quietly in bed for a few minutes more, recalling and relishing each tiny detail as my dream replayed with vivid clarity. I thrilled at the wonder and pristine realness of it all. My whole being was incredibly elated to have not only made contact with my brother Richard, only a few days after his passing on to higher dimensions, but in simultaneously sharing that adventure with my dream girl, which, indeed, was a glorious, added bonus!

Throughout the entire next day I pondered and re-pondered my unique dream. Was it real? Yes. I knew for certain I had broken through "the veil" and that I had rendezvoused with my brother Richard *in spirit!*

Another question arose; what was vitamin K? I had never heard of it! In my limited knowledge then, vitamin E was as high as I thought the vitamin alphabet could go. Partly in curiosity, and partly to double check the reliability of what my brother had communicated

Ellen
Chappelle
Pietsch

to me, I went to the dictionary to see if I could look it up. Sure enough, it was there: "either of two naturally occurring fat-soluble vitamins essential for the clotting of blood." Evidently my system needed it. While growing up, I had many nosebleeds, many without any contact or seeming cause.

The advice was worth following, so I started immediately to eat plenty of dried fruits. I also took the time to soak dried apples in water and drink the juice as a tonic. It tasted great and my health has been superb ever since. Somehow, my spirit-bodied brother really did know something about my body chemistry, the problem, and the natural, healthful cure.

I never realized it that day, but six months later the re-telling of this incredible dream would open wide the door in real physical life for my beloved mate to enter in.

Coincident with all these dream adventures, I was growing more anxious daily to find my real-life soul mate in the physical world! Dreams alone did not cut it. My conscious thrust and resolve in that direction was greatly accentuated and fortified when Mike, a well-known psychic living in Virginia Beach at that time, told me that my long desired mate would enter my life within six months. I had a great fondness and well-deserved confidence in Mike's psychic abilities, so I consequently redoubled my focus and conscious effort to materialize my mate into my life within those six months as she predicted. With much feeling, I "bombarded" my dream mate with silent but potent "broadcasts."

"My beloved one, wherever you are! Listen, I'm in Virginia Beach, Virginia. I'm waiting for you here. Please hurry to my side!"

Gradually, the days weeks and months passed by. The sixth month, July, finally arrived and there was no soul mate in sight. Then on that destined day, the second week of July, my phone rang. I picked up the phone, put the receiver to my ear and said, "hello!"

A pleasant female voice spoke, "I want to place an ad in your paper."

I had recently founded a local newspaper called *The Virginia Beach Free Press*. It was quite literally a one-man operation. I ran all departments; I was publisher, editor, staff writer, typist, lay-out artist, distributor, and ad-taker. I suddenly felt a peculiar and familiar thrill. Nevertheless, displaying as much of a business-like manner as I could muster, I asked her what size and what kind of ad she wanted to place.

"Let me hear your ad," I explained. "That way I can figure out how many words and how much it will cost you."

She said she would be glad to, apparently knowing exactly what she wanted in print.

"A 17x12 inch painting of your dreams for $17.00. That's it," she said.

I questioned my ears. Had I heard her correctly? What kind of a silly-duck-rabbit-goose kind of girl was this!! It was hard to believe. Here was a girl that painted dreams. I caught my breath and smiled. A strange knowing electrical excitement poured through every atom and cell of my being. Ancient memories seemed to surge through my mind. I though silently to myself, "I've got to meet this girl. She sounds like a dream herself!"

Aloud I said, "That's very unusual. So you paint dreams! What else do you do? Are you a writer by any chance?"

"Oh, yes!" she bubbled. "I write about the occult. I'm a dancer. I'm interested in music, and a lot of things!"

"That's great!" I shot back. "You sound very interesting. I would enjoy meeting you in person. Would you mind bringing your ad to me at my office?"

I explained that I ran my newspaper from my home. "The ad will cost you the minimum rate of $2.00. I'll be here working on the paper all afternoon, can you make it?"

"Sure. Give me your address and directions. I'll be there as soon as I get there," she said pleasantly.

Less than twenty minutes later, I looked up from my work to see what appeared to be the most familiar face I had ever seen in my life.

"Hi, I'm Pam, the girl who just called about my ad," said the bell-ringing voice sounding from the bright glowing apparition standing there before me.

"Hello!" I answered. I looked deep into her eyes. "I know you," I said, after several moments of silence. "Probably better than you know yourself!"

Pam looked deep into my eyes in return. I could tell she was searching her mind to see what I was talking about. Nothing registered. Though I had immediately recognized her as my mate, Pam failed to recognize me as the dream lover she had been meeting in dreams for two years. The "mask of clay" we wear physically is far different than the beautiful countenance of the spirit within. Nevertheless, the chemistry was right. There was magic in the air!

We soon began talking animatedly to each other, like lost souls reunited after a long parting. Pam told me she had just arrived that afternoon from Minnesota. She had been prompted to leave Minnesota because she knew she would find her soul mate in Virginia Beach!

Once more, I could hardly believe my ears! I looked her straight in the eyes again and said in my usual forthright manner, "I know. I'm your soul mate!"

A look of surprise flashed across Pam's face. She stared back at me in turn for a long moment, then abruptly shook her head in the negative. She denied the fact vehemently.

"No!" she said, "I have already found him. I ran into him less than an hour ago at the A.R.E. Foundation. His name is Karl!"

I stopped smiling and tried to act unperturbed. Her very matter-of-fact announcement that she belonged to someone else had really surprised me. I knew from my own experience and from observing others how easy it is to deceive ourselves. We try to make a soul mate relationship out of something that does not exist. I recalled that I had tried to make such a relationship to discover later it had all been in my mind. I have talked to others who had done the same thing. Free will can never be abridged. It's simply not possible. There must be a strong magnetic likeness that draws together and creates an equal and balanced interaction at a physical level between true mates. No equal relationship can possibly occur if the "marriage in consciousness" is not there!

In a surprisingly modulated and controlled voice, I explained how I had mistakenly thought certain females I had met were my soul mate. I went on to tell her I knew several other people who had done the same thing and it just doesn't work! I tried to convince her that all of those kind of relationships created in the mind alone would never work out. I avowed emphatically again that this time I knew for certain, beyond any question, that she was truly *my* soul mate! Note that possessiveness there. I told her she would know it for herself when the time was right. I further added a prediction that the bloom would fall off the rose in her sudden meeting with Karl. I said that whatever it was she thought she felt, it was an illusion and would disappear when the glamour of the first meeting wore off.

Naturally, my "raining on her parade" concerning her illusory soul mate link with Karl did not set well with Pam. Nevertheless, I could see she was drawn to stay and talk with me. Some strong form of inner *magnetism* was at work!

Inwardly, I marvelled at my poised, almost miraculous self-control. Her I stood, at long last, in the actual physical presence of my mate. She was the physical reality of the dream lover that I had longed for and dream-loved for two years. I should really be jumping up and down with joy! Even though she had not recognized me, I felt calm and peaceful about it. A silent knowing voice within me said *all was well!*

The inner self knew that both our divine souls and spirits were in control, that our love would surely unfold in due time and in a natural course of unfoldment. That wonderful moment I lived in the *Eternal Now*, that quiet point of rest in the Magnetic Universe where all things extend. The main thing is that she was physically real and now here in my life! That miracle of miracles was astounding and uplifting! The fact that I felt amazingly secure and somehow in full control of the situation, considering the fact that Karl was in Pam's consciousness, was a mystery to me.

Pam and I talked for several hours. My newspaper "work load" was temporarily forgotten. We each revealed our individual beliefs and philosophies to each other. It was no surprise to me that most of our ideas and principles dove-tailed nicely together. With each passing moment, I grew more inwardly pleased over the depth and multicomplexity of the lovely girl-of-my-dreams seated physically before me. I knew beyond any shadow of a doubt that she was my very own appointed and long awaited mate!

When Pam stood to leave, I stepped forward to give her a warm goodbye hug. Politely but firmly she resisted such an immediate close body contact. On her way out, she stopped at the door, gave me a long look and said she would be back to see me again soon.

"Even if you're not my soul mate," she said with a warm impish smile, "You certainly have a very interesting face!"

I thanked her with a silent smile. After she left, I sat and mused to myself that it had been an unusual day, to say the least. I smiled again, perhaps a small fraction of Pam's subconscious mind had tuned in to a recollection that I was the man who had met her so often in dreams. For several minutes I sat quietly, thrilling and tingling warmly with a deep inner wonder and a joyously rich peace. My dreams had literally come true! That beautiful, sensuous dream-mate had physically arrived in my life. It was July. She was at my side. Mike was indeed a good friend, and an accurate psychic, as well. I made it a point to telephone and give her the good news. She was pleased that her prediction had been accurate, and wished me well in the relationship.

Before sleep that evening, I reviewed the day again. My whole being seemed to smile at the next joyous thought. "Pam would soon recognize me fully, as definite and fully as I had recognized her, when the time was right!"

I felt the time was deliciously close. On that grand thought, I fell into a deep, peaceful sleep.

A few nights later Pam stopped by my home and stayed for a long visit again. We spent a leisurely fun-filled night, simply sitting and talking. Her charm and beauty captivated me strongly. Yet, if I made the slightest overture to embrace her, or to even hold her hand, she was always "on guard" and adroitly slipped out of the situation. Each time, she smilingly explained she just wanted to be a friend. Then, when I was just about to give in to a feeling of personal rejection, she turned around and uplifted my spirits greatly. She suddenly admitted in the course of our conversation that she really enjoyed our visits together and would be back again very soon. It was a warm really getting-to-know-you kind of evening. At midnight she left. I walked her to the door. This time she reached out to me and squeezed my hand ever so slightly.

"I had a wonderful time!" she said, as she turned to go.

Knowing I would be seeing her again soon, I went straight to bed and slept peacefully through the night.

To my pleasant surprise, she "dropped in" again the next night for a brief, but wonderful visit. The frequency of her visits increased. Soon Pam was stopping to see me at my work desk several times a day, as well as in the evenings. The subject of Karl was never brought up again by either one of us. I simply acted as if Karl never existed.

It took a lot of self-discipline, but I made the very wise decision not to make any more conscious amorous advances toward her. It was her move next. I reasoned that nature would take its course. The inner enlightenment, or conscious recognition that I was her mate would come to her—and so it did!

The way it came surprised even me. Pam had just gotten back into her car after a late afternoon visit. She had left her briefcase behind, so I quickly ran out to her car, calling out for her to wait. As I smiled and handed her the briefcase, she stared at me as if in a trance. All at once, she drew back from me in fright.

"How did you do that?" she screamed.

I stared back at her wondering what in the world she was talking about!

"How did you do that?" she repeated, demanding to know. I could see a look of pure fright on her face.

"Do what?" I asked, perplexed. I was surprised to see her whole body quivering with fear. I waited for her reply in wonderment.

"You were you, and yet, you weren't you! Your face changed! You were someone else!" she said. Her voice quaked as well. I saw that she was in a state of shock. Her body was now shaking uncontrollably.

I suddenly realized that Pam must have peered through a timewarp, perhaps into another lifetime that we might have shared together in the past. That thought was reinforced when Pam spoke again. This time her voice was much calmer.

"Michael, your face was so different, yet so familiar. It was a face I have known somewhere in another lifetime, I'm sure!"

What a relief!

I found it difficult to conceal my pleasure. I could tell Pam was still somewhat in shock and I knew I had to put her at ease. I put a consoling hand on her shoulder.

"Believe me, Pam," I said, "It wasn't anything I did. You did it. You must have seen a face of what I looked like when we were together in another lifetime all right."

Slowly, Pam gathered herself together. She said it was the most unusual experience of her life and she would never forget it! She turned the car engine back on, leaned out of the window, threw me a kiss, and still wearing a perplexed and awed look, drove slowly away.

As soon as her car was completely out of sight, I literally jumped three feet into the air, with great glee! It was apparent that Pam was on the verge of knowing who I *am*, since she had apparently recalled who I *was!*

That night, immediately on arrival, Pam suggested we go for a quiet walk together on the boardwalk adjacent to the wide and magnificent golden beach. When we arrived at the boardwalk, I took her hand in mine, and this time she did not resist. It seemed that her consciousness and body was tingling just as much as mine was. We walked silently, side-by-side for some time. All at once the same thought arose in both our minds and we expressed it to each other in words with a smile. We acknowledged the ease and naturalness in our rhythmic stride together. It seemed as if we had walked side-by-side, hand-in-hand many, many times before.

As we strolled leisurely along, with one thought we stepped off the boardwalk, took off our shoes and continued onward walking barefooted in the still pleasantly warm golden sands. I looked up and was so thankful for the full moon waxing high above. My soul moved within me and I felt wonderfully romantic. A sudden prompting rose within me to tell Pam about the many unique dreams I had experienced the past two years with my dream girl.

Pam perked up with sudden focused interest. She looked up at me with a warm smile and wide eyes, gently encouraging me to tell her all! We slowed down our pace, and in a soft low voice I told her how the dreams had started. I explained how I had learned to invoke these incredible dreams almost at will, whenever I needed one to uplift me. Pam listened to me quietly, saying nothing, as if she was absorbing every word. When I got to the dream about meeting my brother Richard, soon after his death, Pam suddenly seemed to hang on to every word. While I slowly detailed this extraordinary dream to her, she would stop me from time to time, asking if I would repeat the specific details of certain portions of the dream. I could see she was intensely fascinated. I relished telling her all of the tiniest details of that dream, but I had no idea what she was thinking. When I told her of the exquisite love my dream girl and I had shared so soulfully together as we soared high above the beach on our high flying surfboard, I could feel her hand really tighten in mine.

From Pam's perspective, as she listened to my vivid descriptions of my dream girl encounters, she realized and remembered with growing amazement that she had the same vivid dreams of our encounters together! She recalled her own tremendous feelings of ecstasy, and that great sacred love we shared so often and so blissfully in our dream states together!

The sudden shock seemed almost too much for her mind and soul to assimilate in that moment. She explained to me later that it had been a supreme effort to keep from blurting out that she was my dream lover. The other conservative part of her felt she dare not, that she needed to hold that knowledge within her as sacred and sweetly as she could for the time being. She said she wanted to think about it, to ponder it in the silence of her own mind before she shared such bombastic news with me. She admitted she knew then why she, too, had felt such a strong familiarity with me. She was glad that our love had developed so naturally between us, without ever having to go to bed together! Pam felt if I knew that she knew she was my soul mate or dream lover, as a male I would push immediately for a physical sex relationship with her.

Back to me. That long walk and talk seemed to have brought about the great miracle I had been waiting for. The impenetrable wall that had seemed to separate Pam and me was gone. She had drawn closer and closer to me in spirit, soul, and body! At that point, I did not know the rest of the story.

That night, when we parted, Pam gave me a warm hug and invited me to come to her apartment on Sunday evening for a home-cooked dinner. I accepted her invitation with great joy, promising to bring along the best bottle of red wine I could find for the occasion. After she left, I could feel wave after wave of happiness and peace beyond understanding grow within my being. Though she had not yet admitted it, I sensed she already knew we were mates. The next evening, I learned how knowing my intuition had been.

Pam and I had been seeing a lot of each other—every day for several weeks. When I arrived home after receiving my invitation to dinner with her, I made a sudden out-of-character decision. It was still three days and nights before Sunday. I decided my best bet to get Pam to really want my company would be for me to play hard to get. The next two days I would pretend to be too busy to visit or be visited. That should work.

Something worked! Pam did not come over for her daily visit and the day seemed to drag by endlessly. By mid-afternoon I could hardly stand it. My entire being literally ached to be with her, to see her face and touch her physically. I reminded myself that I was playing hard to get and a huge internal mind/feeling battle began. It was a mighty one. The more I centered my mind on the seemingly cold clear logic of staying away from Pam, the more my feelings flamed and burned and protested to see her immediately. Before long I knew my desire to be with her was so much stronger that I decided to surrender to those loving feelings! Logical or not, my soul and spirit knew that a pure warm loving experience now was a thousand times more important than any cold, though even undebatably accurate theory of how to achieve it later!

I quickly followed my pounding heart and was soon in my car driving straight for her apartment. Pam acted surprised, but also showed great pleasure at my unexpected visit. All day long, her soul had been processing the new knowledge about our relationship. She was wondering about the best way to tell me about it.

After we sat down to talk, Pam told me she actually had been sitting alone all day, yearning to see me. This is a clear example of how the same strong inner desire flaming between two people eventually bridges time and space. She made coffee, and as we sipped the brew we talked about little things. Then suddenly, she dropped the bombshell!! I was totally unprepared for it. She took my hand and caressed it lovingly while a smile formed sweetly on her lips.

"What would you do," she said, "If I told you I am the girl you met in your dreams?"

There was a warm glowing light of love shining in her eyes. My heart started to pound with excitement. She continued to talk and my excitement kept mounting. I leaned forward, closer, almost to the edge of my chair. The tables were now reversed. It was me who was hanging on every word!

"Do you mean to tell me," I broke in, "that we both were dreaming the same dream together, that you actually dreamed the same dream I did?"

"Yes," Pam nodded. "I remember being with you in several of your dreams, especially in your dream about your brother Richard. I remembered you had not seen your brother for several years before he died. I stood by the gate when you went into the light to see him. I was so afraid you were going to stay too long. I felt if you didn't return soon, you might die, and I would never see you again. I was so happy when I saw you coming back to me!"

Pam lowered her voice almost to a whisper and spoke with great feeling as she lost herself in my eyes.

"I remember so clearly how much I loved you in my dreams, and how truly heavenly I felt soaring through the air on that narrow surfboard with your strong arms wrapped around me. I felt so good when you snuggled close!"

A divine moment later we were entwined again, ecstatically wrapped in each other's arms! That same memorable holy glow that I thrilled to in my dreams repeated itself and flooded both of our blissful beings! Long into that destined night we touched, caressed, kissed, and lost ourselves in exquisitely physical and heavenly embraces. Those same ecstatic male-female feelings I had felt so frequently in my dreams became a sensuous and earthy reality that wondrous evening.

For days, weeks, and months, we shared a growing spiritual and physical love. Neither possessed the other. New decisions in life come, and side-by-side adventures, no matter how desirable at certain levels, may conclude. *We had both desired strongly to share a mating at the level of soul with our opposite mate. It became our reality.* It soon became obvious that other realities between us needed con frontation. Pam's interests and life mission were far different than mine. She shared little or no interest in my "spiritual" work, nor in my books or lectures. Her dreams and passions inevitably led her upon her path and mine took me on another. That is precisely the way it was and needed to be.

One enlightening day we both knew and acknowledged that our adventure together in this lifetime had ended. We released each other from within the light of our souls and parted our physical pathways. However, appearances are deceiving. Even better things were ahead for both of us. What looked like the end was just the beginning!

3

What Is a Soul Mate?

Of all the magnificent stars in the sky,
where is that one that knows I?

Exactly what is a soul mate? My definition may be totally different
from one given by another. It is very important that you and I know
what we are talking about together. For now, the most concise,
direct definition of a soul mate is a mate you meet at a soul level.

That brings up an immediate question. What's different about
meeting someone at the level of the soul, rather than just person to
person? In fact, what exactly is a soul level, compared to any other
conceivable level where we could meet with someone else? The
answer to these questions will give us comprehension of what holds
or separates any relationship. Two or more people can meet at several
known levels—physically, emotionally, mentally or spiritually.

A physical-to-physical meeting between two persons is understood by everyone. It's basic and necessary if exchanges are to be
made between one person and another in our three-dimensional
world. A mind-to-mind kind of rapport with another is also easily
identified. Two people who are both heavily polarized mentally can
carry on lengthy interchanges about what each one thinks, believes,
or occasionally knows. The emotional or spiritual levels are more
difficult to understand. However, when two individuals both love

to watch sunsets and sunrises, or like to listen to the same kind of music, or like to read the same kind of poetry, and love identical art expressions, it means they essentially feel what the other one feels. Meeting at some feeling levels is vitally essential in all lasting relationships. Through more refined feelings or new sensitivities, the evolution of body consciousness is advanced. That is the vital difference between the individual who hears a Beethoven concert and hears only the notes, while another hears and feels the immortality of the soul and is greatly uplifted. The inner sensitivity of the soul is vastly different than the purely frictional or electric sensations of the body.

Normally, we meet all people in varying degrees at each of these three levels, physically, mentally, or emotionally. We can rightly call this unified meeting of all three levels between ourselves and another a meeting between personalities. Each person's personality has three distinctive and identifiable elements within it. These triune factors are a physical presence, a thought or thinking presence, and a feeling or emotional presence. Because our physical mass or cellular structure works through electrical reflexes called instinct, it can be said that thoughts, feelings, and instincts comprise the sum total of our personality.

Since everything in nature reflects duality, I point out that the personality nature represents a *negative* aspect of our being, while the soul or inner spirit represents the *positive* nature within us. Our personality reflects the Electric Universe and the soul and spirit reflects the still Magnetic Universe. Psychologically, these two are of necessity opposites. The electric universe confines us to the involutionary process, while the magnetic universe connects us to the evolutionary forward advancing and uplifting aspect of nature. The individual personality, or soul force, shows itself in countless obvious ways. The negative expressions of personality are opposed to the positive expressions of the soul. Knowing this leads us to the understanding that in any relationship, if one party is acting predominately like a sleeping personality and the other is functioning as an awakened soul, a common meeting point between them exists only through the soul-infused entity.

The greater can contain the lesser, but the lesser cannot contain the greater. The person who is conscious from the soul perspective can meet and understand the person coming from the lesser viewpoint. However, the lesser cannot contain the greater, so the personality-oriented individual cannot meet or comprehend the other awakened person that comes from the soul. Another corresponding way to look at this is that you can pour a pint (a personality) into a quart (a soul), but you cannot pour a quart into a pint. It simply cannot contain it! The quart-sized soul knows the pint-sized personality, but that same enlightened knowingness is impossible in reverse.

Some of the basic characteristics of the personality (sometimes known as the alter-ego) is that it is fearful, doubtful, and expresses only conditioned or possessive love. It is defiant, competitive, defensive, guilty, and insecure, just to mention a brief few of its negative traits. On the other hand, the positive virtues of the soul (sometimes known as the ego) are just the opposite. An individual imbued with soul power lacks fear, expresses confidence, and gives unconditioned love freely. She or he acts in a receptive, cooperative, open and secure way, without guilt or insecurity. Nothing needs to be proved, it simply is.

In pursuing a dual viewpoint, almost unlimited simple dualities could be listed, corresponding exactly to the very real negative presence of an alter-ego or personality and the precise opposite positive presence of soul force. It is worth repeating: the soul is not only more expansive and inclusive, but it is tremendously more powerful than the personality. "May the force be with you," popularized in the *Star Wars* movies means exactly that! Soul power is more than a phrase or slogan; it is a creative, loving reality waiting to awaken within the conscious reality of everyone.

I now add that spirit is the greatest aspect of our individual trinity. It can and does literally contain both soul and personality within it. Though soul is infused by spirit, and can and does contain personality, as already pointed out, it cannot contain the vastness of spirit. Eventually, the sleeping personality can be awakened and incorporated consciously into the soul as a positive three-dimensional tool. Until then, though, the sleeping personality consciousness only identifies and relates to all the other billions of present-day personalities on earth. Thus, one last time, personality cannot contain either soul or spirit, but it is always infused by some degree with soul and spirit. Otherwise it would cease to exist in a physical world.

Therefore, that great standard for measuring, "By their fruits they shall be known," applies here. You can wisely weigh the ideas and actions of others and know how little or how much divinity is showing. Blind narrow-minded belief about anything, because someone said God said it, does not pass muster anymore! It is not the ignorant person who claims something for nothing salvation, who beats the breast and proclaims a holier-than-thou attitude that demonstrates soul-force. It is just the opposite! It is the uncondi-tioned, loving and allowing person, tolerant of the ideas and thoughts of another, who expresses genuine soul quality. Look and know for yourself. It is the positive or negative words, or lack of them—the positive or negative thoughts and feelings, or lack of them—the positive or negative physical actions—or lack of them, that displays clearly to any objective viewer whether an awakened soul, or a soundly sleeping personality, is in charge and present.

You can recognize which of these vast differences in life expression you are choosing at this moment. If you don't like what you see, simply change it. Obviously, when you can discern these differences and sources of expression, whether in yourself or in others, you are at a great advantage. You know exactly where that person "is coming from" and can handle it appropriately.

To sum up these insights, when any two people meet at the soul level of consciousness, there is an automatic recognition and blend. That instant kind of divine communion, literally the language of light, can happen between strangers, friends, business associates, family and loved ones. If that meeting is between single mates, then a real soul mate relationship is already there according to this first definition of soul mates.

Later in this volume, we will address the terms *twin-souls, twin-flames, kindred souls, astrological twins,* and other such words invented to carry the idea of special or unique male/female relationships. There are many terms used to convey this idea of an extraordinary affinity between opposite sexes.

Having the divine presence of someone in your life who is your equal, whether called a soul mate, or identified by any other unique label, is a joyful and most blessed time on this earth. Many people are depressed because they do not have one. If you are the romantic type, then your pain burns even greater when your hours are spent alone. Having spent the greater part of my teenage and adult lifetime as one of these romantic types, I know. Not loving or being loved by a mate of the opposite sex seemed so unnatural to me. I realize there are some human beings who do not need or desire that exquisite joy of warm companionship and love shared with a marriage partner at the soul level—or even at any other level. Some people are happily married to their jobs, their careers, to their art, to their politics, to their religion, to their science, to their business, to their family, to their nation, or best of all, to their God! They are holding a one-pointed focus on their vision or mission in life chosen by them. There is nothing wrong with that. They are doing and enjoying what makes them happy and what is right for the moment, thus speeding up their own evolution. These aforementioned individuals have chosen a destiny to be alone. Ultimately, each one of us must meet our God alone, face to face. It can't be done "holding hands" with a soul mate.

In this lifetime I have chosen to be a family man, meaning to be with a mate that I love and who loves me. What do you choose?

Since you are reading this volume, I assume you want to manifest "someone special" into your life, someone who can love as you love, live as you live, and dream as you dream. Great! Then I know how to help you speed onward to that divine destiny!

As a rule, a "family situation" of marriage and children is the very best ground available for sowing the seeds of self-maturity and soul-growth. In a marriage situation, a man and a woman are tested daily and are able to evolve many times daily. The simple act of overcoming a physical or mental problem individually or together enriches soul-growth. Think about it. Anyone who is in your life, and who acts like a perfect mirror, can reflect back to you all your great strengths and weaknesses. Since no one can grow when he or she is ignorant of weaknesses, your "equal" is literally a God-send!

Focus on and follow your desire to find your soul mate. A strong desire gives you invincible power. I wish you God-speed as you explore these thoughts and put them to action. You are on a divinely blessed and holy journey!

4

Is There More Than One?

Extend and unite in warm embrace, reach out, expand and touch all your other points and parts in space.

Count the stars in the heavens. Is there more than one heaven? Indeed there are. For some it is theory; for me it is fact that for each tiny or huge star in whatever universe, there is always another star which is an exact counterpart. In that unlimited void of all existence, there are countless other life forms in addition to our own unique humanoid structures, and they are also involving and evolving, unfolding and refolding, compressing and expanding, descending and ascending, all in their own times and seasons, within their own time shared "frame" of space.

Why would such an unlimited Creator-of-all-that-is not create countless matches or counterparts, one of the other, so that recognition and inner growth between them could occur? Unless all mates were equally balanced by a counter-mate, the entire universe would be out of balance!

Think about it. Keep thinking it through. Why are you so attracted to some people and so repulsed by others? Why do you sense an immediate familiarity, or a sisterhood or brotherhood with some individuals you meet on sight? Simply because there are

Ellen
Chappelle
Pietsch

matching wavelengths, tones, sounds, light spectrums, thoughts, or ideas that match. Just think about the overwhelming mathematical odds at work. There are now over six and a half billion human souls on earth today! If only one in ten thousand were at the same soul awareness level as yourself, the so-called right age, right appearance, and so on, then there are now at least 650,000, with half of them male or female. This leaves 325,000 possible soul mate matches, providing you are able to meet your opposite at a soul level. This affords a wide range of possible soul mates, you must agree!

What if there were only one person in a million that resonated at your pitch or soul level? That still leaves over 3,000 wonderful alignments around. Let us be so incredulous as to suggest that perhaps only one in a billion vibrates with you at your soul altitude. That still gives you at least three soul mates to choose from.

Put aside any fears that you have been left "out in the cold" or that no one on earth could love or understand you. All of us have plenty of company at whatever relatively high or low level of the soul we are operating with. Since all levels of the soul are positive, then no matter at what level, the very lowest of the low, or the highest of the high, there is an equal someone to mirror back your own divine identity. Give thanks and focus on that thought whenever needed in the future as well.

Meanwhile, doesn't it seem wise to leave all fears, doubts, guilts, or other self-created stumbling blocks you may have adopted somewhere and sometime in the past behind? Simply know you have all of the faculties and factors at work within you to summon at will your soul mate to you.

Ponder this. Are you alive and conscious of that aliveness? Do you really have choice or free will? Do you have an open mind which makes anything possible? Only a closed mind is impossible! Do you desire? If so, you have all the power of the universe within you at your command to call forth and materialize your soul mate into your reality. Desire is the sole source of all power!

Realize beyond any doubt that there is someone right now who is your ideal counterpart wanting to know you and be with you at this exact moment. Be fully assured—your equal wants to be with you as much as you want to be with him or her. Armed with this knowledge, proceed light-heartedly on your magnificent journey. Whatever you know absolutely is absolute!

5

How Soul-Mate
Relationships Begin

The daisies never tell. Lift your wondering eyes to the heavens.
There the one star will appear!

The how, as well as the where, a soul mate relationship develops comes from several factors. Whether you believe the Earth is round, or not, doesn't change the fact that it is, even though many people thought it was flat for thousands of years. Whether you believe in reincarnation, or not, doesn't change the fact. If reincarnation is not within your reality, it simply means that false beliefs or teachings have been accepted, and you have not yet found supportive facts to convince you that all human souls come and go into human form again and again. This process simply continues endlessly until you and I arrive at the same soul awakened identity that Jesus found 2,000 years ago. Only when we know that "the kingdom of heaven is within" or "My father and I are one" does the reincarnation cycle cease at the human level. There is no condemnation of your belief if reincarnation is not yet your belief or knowingness. Each soul alone is responsible for what it believes or knows. I would point out however, that, as long as you believe in anything, you can be manipulated, herded, or driven in any direction while those in power feed you empty beliefs. The best position of consciousness concerning anything is to know. Knowing is the God-quality of the soul and of the magnetic universe, while believing and thinking are qualities of personality and of the limited electric universe. Isn't it wise to move consciously out of the "belief systems" fed to all of us immersed in social consciousness and live instead only by what we know? Admittedly, that is a big switch. The immediate rewards of growth far outweigh the cost of leaving old dogma behind. The truth always sets you free!

Reincarnation sometimes plays a "heavy hand" in why some soul mates are drawn to each other at first glance. We have all been born and reborn in all the major civilizations upon Earth. Each time in each lifetime when a close bond of love or hate has been set up between two people, it is recorded in both souls. Nothing is ever forgotten once it has been experienced by any form of consciousness. In this one area alone, we may have a huge pool of lives with lovers. This is why when someone from a past lifetime enters a room or walks before us, there is an innate recognition, a pleasant—or sometimes quite unpleasant—familiarity.

It follows then, if we had a wonderful rapport with that person in a past lifetime, it would be easy if all conditions are also favorable, to re-enter another relationship based on soul memory. It works the other way around as well. Someone we despised or hated in another lifetime may again appear to us so that we may now learn what is also lovable about them. We can behold God within anything or anyone if we only look deep enough.

In some cases, the past relationship stands as a plateau or base from which we can keep on growing more. A past marriage partner may feel that here has been unfinished business between him or her and self. In that event, the current relationship may last only long enough to clear up the old business and then end abruptly. Free will, choice, and focus, are always determining factors. If, on the other hand, the meeting of the souls moves forward together at that high level between them, they may wind up creating an enduring soul mate relationship. You both have chosen to pursue the same path, side-by-side, to grow toward God-hood together.

Anyone who takes a realistic look at the state of the world today can see for themselves that almost all marriage relationships are confined to personality exchanges. That strong glue of magnetism, or soul force, is almost non-existent. Thus, what appears to be a seemingly solid relationship soon becomes shaky, falters, and leads to a parting of the ways. There was a time when I believed that marriages should end between marriage partners if mental, emotional, physical, or spiritual differences seemed incompatible. My knowingness now is that all marriages must be considered sacred and, once entered into, should not be terminated for any reason except physical, mental, or emotional abuse.

In light of this, is it possible to be married to someone who does not appear to be your soul mate to begin with, but who may become one through years of patient tolerance and allowing with each other? Yes. With God, what's impossible?

It follows, that if you have not yet already done so yourself, you must also lift up your consciousness or awareness to meet your mate at a soul plateau. Unless both of you are communicating and interacting together on the same "frequency band," that blissful soul unity you could share is not possible. Expressed in a slightly different way, it is only through a soul-consciousness that mates share that the term soul mates becomes applicable, as presently defined. When we have earned the privilege of meeting a marriage partner at soul levels, during any one incarnation together, that possibility then goes on record and extends into any future lifetime of meeting and sharing together again! This does not mean you must be legally or formally married according to the custom of the land. The real marriage between any two entities always exists within consciousness between them. If you are truly married to another, you will know it, and will enjoy your relationship as such. If not, the marriage has not been there to begin with and needs to be created if you are already married. The marriage must be between yourself and your mate. The marriage papers merely represent legal intimidation of a mocking ritual and worthless paper promises. It is only the inner laws established by the very God of our inner being that create and govern a true marriage, not the rulers of the land or priestly man-made rituals. The unique form any marriage takes varies from nation to nation, region to region, race to race, and religion to religion, but the mutual unified-consciousness aspect of a marriage agreement between female and male in any country, region, race, or religion is ever the same. It is, or it isn't! The wedding must first take place as an agreement mutually shared in consciousness. Then only may the marriage genuinely reflect some sort of outer act or physical fusion. All such marriages are sacred and should never be dissolved for any reason except violent abuse of one by the other.

Holding your marriage together sacredly once it has been established is extremely important. Adultery is a very real violation of God's laws even if the adultery is committed only in the mind. We can make any existing marriage or male-female affinity a very real soul mate relationship if we choose! That may require a considerable amount of will power and disciplined soul force, but the rewards are sublime. Therefore, once we are willing and able to raise our present day relationship to a soul level, whether that be a common-law marriage, or any other outward manner of fusion, we will find ourselves interacting happily with our soul mate, right where we stand in the Eternal Now!

Of course, this new consciousness means a change of self through changes of attitude. It will also take time and effort, for it is always difficult to confront or bypass our own rigid personality beliefs and *allow* others theirs. Very few of us have learned to some degree how to allow others their own ideas of truth, no matter how limited it appears, or is known to us. Consciously bringing to bear a positive allowing soul force into our interchanges unites and uplifts that relationship, whether with a marriage partner, a business partner, a stranger, a friend, or loved family members.

Fortunately, our almighty souls do have the power to influence, act upon us, impress, or direct our sleeping personality consciousness into physical action contrary to or beyond a chosen thought or feeling. The "inner self" can veto a direction chosen by our personality. Our personality may decide on a certain course of action, or line of direction, and our soul can step in and override that decision. At will, our soul can lead us toward an entirely different pathway or outcome when it is more fulfilling to the God within us. That "divine intervention," or act of taking charge at an unexpected moment in our lives, is a direct application of that universal law touched upon briefly earlier, "the greater controls the lesser." I know, I've experienced it several times already.

The following account, a true story of how my soul took charge and altered the course of my footsteps and destiny, will help convey this idea to you. This story also demonstrates that even between true mates, a great enough friction can cause a rift, or time/space separation between them. Therefore, if you have ever wondered whether it is possible to have a break-up in a relationship between soul mates, the answer is *yes!* Any powerful imbalance or mis-use of energy and consciousness on the physical plane can disrupt your life immensely. I know this for a fact.

Very early in my professional basketball career, I met and married a lovely girl, who was definitely "my equal," if not far more soul-infused than myself at that time. I literally drove her out of my life through one, explosive, insanely jealous violent act.

The two of us had just finished a loud shouting war when my unthinking act of violence endangered her life greatly. At the peak of this violent emotional drama, time stood still. My anger had provoked me into slamming my fist into her stomach. Less than two weeks prior to that, Bonnie had undergone an appendix operation. I literally could have killed her with that blow.

My act was actually almost a perfect *time reflex mirrored reaction,* when Bonnie, through the same kind of insane jealousy, had stabbed me in the stomach with a dagger, causing my instant death, in a lifetime less than 5,000 years before. It was during a lifetime we shared then in Hawaii. The past is the past, and the present is the present. I had at that precise moment in this lifetime, committed an almost identical violent action against her. The door of time opened wide again. The small living room vanished from sight. An awesome crystal-clear vision appeared in its place. Now, my beautiful Bonnie changed before my eyes into a haggard old woman. She stood bathed in an eerie pink fiery glow, wrinkled with the dust and age of time. The aging process accelerated! I watched in total horror as she began to crack and disintegrate rapidly, leaving only a foot-high heap of ashen grey dust before my eyes.

Simultaneously, a stern voice spoke aloud inside my consciousness. The mysterious voice announced my unbalanced violent physical act of jealous rage against Bonnie had just created an immense uncrossable rift between her soul and mine. The inner voice stated that the breach would continue to exist between her soul and mine until I saw this very same vision repeated once more before my eyes. The voice said we would part our ways within days. My soul had intervened. The promise it made to repeat the macabre vision was kept many years later.

As the spectacular scene vanished, I again became aware of standing in the living room before a shocked Bonnie. Her face was ashen and she was doubled over in pain from my sudden explosive and totally unexpected blow. I stood there silently for a long moment. My anger had left me. I was stark sober now and frozen in time. I shook with fear and was filled with immediate great remorse and great apprehension. I knew Bonnie could die before my eyes.

She was terribly ill for a few minutes, but gradually recovered her breath and her composure. The battle had ended in unexpected violence. Both of us were greatly shaken and held each other wordlessly for several moments. The mystery of that eerie time-warp vision remained unsolved right up until the very last moment, when that exact vision repeated itself in detail before my eyes, exactly as foreordained by my God within.

Meanwhile, the passionate love relationship of the past soured between my beloved Bonnie and myself. In quick, successive, explosive events, Bonnie and I were soon separated and divorced. The prediction had become a reality. I was alone again in the world. Everything previously meaningful in my life had suddenly collapsed upon me. I nevertheless continued to feel a strong and yearning love for Bonnie. But an impenetrable wall suddenly came between us. No matter how hard I tried, I could not locate a new physical address for her or discover her physical presence. For ten long, soulfully painful years, I mentally, and sometimes even physically, chased the ghost of my "lost love." Every female form seen from a distance that looked like it might be her quickened my attention and hopes. Again and again these continued self-delusions proved disappointingly wrong every time. It seemed as if she had vanished off the face of the earth. I knew that her parents knew where she was, but they refused to tell me, so the invisible but mighty barrier remained between us. I still kept right on hoping and searching, as one by one, the long searching years passed by. Fortunately, even though my head was turned and stretched back to the past a lot, I managed to find some "now time" and a few personal breakthroughs in my own understanding of reality.

At another time, when I attempted to leave civilization and live the rest of my life in a cave, that same stern voice spoke. Time stopped momentarily again. *The voice* informed me that I could not vegetate, hiding away in a cave, that I must immediately make my way back to civilization and gather more self-knowledge, sharing it with others as I learned to digest and live it. I had gone to "The Valley of the Lost Tribe" in Kauai, The Garden Island of Hawaii. My feeling was that all of Earth was completely uncivilized and barbaric, and I no longer wished to live in such a hostile environment. My full intent was to live out the rest of my days in the seclusion of the huge cave I had just discovered along the beach side of the valley. Instead, I turned back as directed, totally turned around in a new direction. This time, I was a man with a mission. With an open mind, I sought for knowledge wherever I could find it. Since knowledge wants to be grabbed or seized as much as we want to grab or seize it, I found my way from teacher to teacher, always advancing a little more as I mastered each new school of thought presented to me.

Back to Bonnie. Ten years later my endless quest for truth brought me to an extraordinary teacher who presided over a Religious Science Church in southern California. We can call him Lew and thus preserve his identity.

Lew had twenty or so new students studying his advanced training course in healing. He handed each of us a small slip of white paper. Lew instructed us to write down whatever it was that we wanted most of all in life, just that one desired thing on the paper. Then he told us to put our initials on the bottom, fold it up and place it back into the collection bowl that he was holding. He waited patiently while we wrote down our individual desires, then collected

them and passed the bowl around the room again. He said our weekend home assignment was to draw out one of the slips. When we got home, we were instructed to read what our brothers or sisters in the class had written down as their burning desires. Our job would be to put our training into practice. Each one of us would focus on seeing the reality of the desire written down in our mind's eye for a few hours over the weekend. It was our task to help make whatever desire we had selected from the bowl a concrete living reality. It was the start of a great game and all of us went home feeling very enthused and excited about our home assignment. The "twist" of helping another get what he or she wanted added to the intrigue.

That weekend, following instructions from Lew, I sat down to focus on what seemed to me to be a tremendously frivolous desire from a female classmate. No matter how hard I tried, I could not really get serious about helping someone manifest such a seemingly worthless desire. Nevertheless, I kept up a half-hearted attempt to focus on that whimsical wish.

All at once, I seemed to be hit on the head by meaningful moving thought. If I was finding it hard to focus on manifesting the idea belonging to someone else, then chances are whoever had received my desire might be making the same half-hearted attempt! I suddenly made a firm decision to be responsible for my own creating work. Why should I depend on someone else doing my job for me?

My own desire was expressed in a brief but vitally meaningful message. "I want to make contact with B.B. again!"

That had been the one prevalent thought and desire within me for almost ten years. I wanted that more than anything else at that moment! The more I thought about it, the stronger grew my resolve to make it happen. I would do it myself, not through the power of another!

Up until then, it had appeared to be impossible. Not one of the many letters to Bonnie's parents had ever been acknowledged. They had not been returned to me, so it seemed reasonable to assume the letters had been received. At that moment, I felt invincible. I was inspired to sit down and write a long pleading letter, first to Bonnie's parents, and then to Bonnie, in care of them. I knew that since her parents would not let me have Bonnie's address, I would really have to be persuasive if I expected them to reply to my letter. Somehow, I knew this letter would finally get through to Bonnie. What you know absolutely is absolute!

In my letter to her parents, I explained that I was a new person. I told them I had recently found an inspiring new spirituality within. I poured out my love from the soul to them, while also pouring out my deep remorse and anguish over losing Bonnie. I acknowledged full blame for our separation and asked their forgiveness for making their daughter unhappy. I shamelessly begged them to pass the enclosed letter to Bonnie, inviting them to read it first if they chose.

When that long letter was finished, I began another, as equally wordy but charged with soul force and love to Bonnie. I asked for her forgiveness, expressing my eternal love and a desire to see her again.

When the last word of both letters was written I felt so incredibly excited and exalted. I felt as if I had already made connection somehow and the rest would simply soon be history. This proved to be quite a valid insight.

I had hardly laid my pen down and sealed the envelope when another positive thought impressed my mind. I felt an irresistible urge to get into my car and pop the letter into the mailbox at the main street of the shopping mall in Redondo Beach, very near where I lived then. Without hesitation, I jumped into my car with letter in hand and sped for the mall. As I neared my destination, I parked my car and walked over to the mailbox. I kissed the fat, already stamped letter a final goodbye and God-speed. The moment the letter disappeared into the blue U.S. mailbox an astounding burst of energy poured through me. I felt mightily uplifted. I could leap tall buildings with one mighty bound! Along with it came another provocative thought. For several days, I had wanted to treat myself to a movie featuring one of my favorite actors, Robert Mitchum. I decided to do it immediately. The movie house was nearby, but it was further away than I wanted to walk. I strode back to my car feeling ten feet tall. It seemed almost as if my body had no weight, as if I was walking on air. With spirits soaring, I got into my car and drove straight for the busy cross-street where the Robert Mitchum movie was showing.

"It's finished," I spoke mentally to myself. "This time I know my letter is getting through to Bonnie!"

Without any pre-signal or warning, the strong hand of my soul was placed on my shoulder. I was nearing the busy intersection, but instead of driving straight ahead and turning into the parking lot, I abruptly swung my car into another theater's parking lot on my right. This absolutely was the wrong theater! Or was it! I was dumb-founded.

"Why did I do that?" I asked myself. *No answer!*

I turned my head to look up and read the movie marquee above the ticket booth. The movie title, *She*[2] registered vaguely in my now half-frozen consciousness. One part of me could not fathom what I was doing, while another unknown part of me seemed to be in charge and knew exactly what it wanted! I had no conscious intention to park in *that* lot and go to *that* movie. Until that precise moment I had not even known that a movie by that name existed, though I was aware of the small theater on that corner. What happened? I was supposedly heading for the other movie starring Robert Mitchum. I had no intention of seeing another movie. I had not only turned and parked in the *wrong* movie parking lot, but I was getting out of my car and walking to the *wrong* ticket booth, to buy a ticket for the *wrong* movie!

Rebellious thoughts flashed through my mind like popcorn popping.

"What is this? What's going on? Why am I doing this?" *No answer.*

---

[2] The movie "She" is based on a novel of the same name by H. Rider Haggard, originally published in 1887, and available as a reprint from several publishers. Check your local library. The movie, first made in 1917, was remade several times throughout the years. This British version of the movie was made in 1965.

This was a case where truth was greater than fiction. I arrived at the ticket booth, pushed the correct amount of money to the ticket agent, and the smiling young lady handed me my ticket. She urged me to hurry and turn down the far aisle since the movie was about to begin. All the while, an eerie feeling that I had lost my mind somewhere was gripping me.

"Why was I deliberately going against what I thought I wanted to do?" I enquired. *Still no answer.*

I turned down the far aisle as directed and slipped into the first seat that was vacant. The moment I sat down, the movie lights turned out and the screen lights flashed on. It was split-second timing, as if some unseen entities had flashed a signal to other unseen entities who turned off the lights and turned on the movie.

Perhaps by now, you can realize how bewildered and tense I was as I sat watching the movie credits flash on and the movie begin.

As the main characters appeared on the screen above me the eerie sensation grew. The lead actor in the movie, John Richardson, was an almost exact look-alike of myself at that time. He had the same skin coloring, the same poise, or aura about him as mine, the same build and height, the same blue eyes, the same abundant crop of hair and the same somewhat arrogant bearing I often displayed in my walk or body postures. I had the distinct odd sensation I was watching myself on the screen. *I was about to get my answer!*

The plot swiftly unfolded. It dealt with a "lost civilization" ruled by a cruel but beautiful queen, who seemingly possessed immortal life and thus, unlimited power over her subjects. Three friends recently discharged from the Foreign Legion were planning to find that lost city to bring back all of the legendary treasure they could carry. As their excitement for the great adventure grew, so did my own. I was one with them. Each unfolding movement of the movie seemed to be leading me toward some kind of dramatic explosion.

When the lead actress, played by Ursula Andress, appeared, I sat forward on the edge of my seat with unbelieving eyes. She was the counterpart of Bonnie! She had the same incredible figure, the long blonde hair, and the sand-green-blue eyes. From that moment, I never left the front edge of my seat until the entire performance was over. My entire being was engulfed in sensing, feeling, living the dramatic saga unfolding before my wondering, staring eyes.

The setting in the movie switched to the secluded valley where the goddess Queen ruled over her subjects with an iron, tyrannical hand. The Queen had killed her former lover, the King, now reincarnated many thousands of years later as one of the three friends, while in a jealous fit over his affair with a slave girl. *She plunged a dagger into his belly and he died immediately.* The Queen was filled with remorse, for she truly loved the King, knowing he had no other equal on Earth. Shortly after his murder, she found the secret of immortality, but refused to share it with anyone else, since it made her invincible. She yearned to be back in the arms of the King, and since she was immortal, she knew it was simply a matter of time until he would reincarnate on Earth again. When the three adventurers were making their plans, she traveled to the city and engaged him directly. She told the reincarnated King the story of their past and invited him to come back to her. She revealed that many men had desired to be her King during his long absence, but she had found them all unworthy. He must again prove his own worthiness. Only if he succeeded in making the long trek across mountains and burning deserts to the Valley of the Lost Civilization without aid from guides would he be allowed entrance into her Kingdom. She gave him a map, kissed him goodbye, and told him she would be eagerly awaiting his return. She disappeared as mysteriously as she had appeared.

The reincarnated King, followed closely by his two companions, battled man and nature but finally arrived triumphantly at the lost valley. He was received with great joy by the wicked Queen. She told him in the course of events that he, too, could learn the secret of immortality, and together they would rule the world. She invited him into the secret mountain chamber to go through the eternal ritual with her. While her King-to-be watched, the Queen stepped upon a round stone altar. She explained that only once in a thousand years a certain key star in the heavens would be in exactly the correct position so that a ray of its eerie light shone through a hole in the mountainside and upon the altar. She said the altar would soon spring into harmless flames. She had danced in those flames 5,000 years before and they had given her physical immortality. She wanted her King to have the same, and stepping onto the altar as the flames arose to begin the dance, she invited him to join her. The flames licked and swirled around her while the King watched in wonder.

Suddenly, the Queen screamed in horrible pain. There was sudden fear and terror in her eyes. Before the King could make a move, she froze in position while the flames consumed her!

I leaned forward further in my seat and gasped in astonishment. I had stepped through the doorway of time! Here now, on the screen before my physical eyes, as promised by my soul, that exact same vision that had occurred ten years ago was repeating itself. Tears gushed to my eyes, as B.B., a dazzling beauty only a few seconds before, was transformed into a wrinkled dry hag. The scars of time, the transgressions of the ages, became visibly incorporated into her body. Gradually, the entire body shrunk, consumed into a foot high heap of smoldering ashes.

My heart thumped and pounded. The rest of the cinema went by unnoticed. My eyes poured rivers of tears, but inside, my whole being reeled with divine delight! A sweet joy supernal sang within my soul. The promise made had been kept. I had just seen the long ago predicted vision repeated before my eyes. It was a welcome omen that my reunion with Bonnie had been re-established.

Interestingly, a time lag ensued. My letter was not "passed on" to Bonnie until two years later. She called me instantly after reading the letter.

Her mother, June, called me as soon as my letter arrived and she and my ex-father-in-law had read it. She told me Bonnie had just accepted an offer of marriage to a very nice man from a wealthy family. She said the man who Bonnie was marrying was my look-alike. However, she said that Bonnie had never gotten over her love for me fully, and that if she gave Bonnie my letter at that time, Bonnie would probably not go ahead with the marriage. She asked me to think about it for a while and give her my decision when I was ready. She would do what I asked.

I knew that I wanted only the best for Bonnie, and with a heavy heart I told June to wait until Bonnie was well into her marriage before she passed my letter along. She had waited two years, but the communication got through the Electric Universe, despite the time lag. It was wonderful to talk with Bonnie again. We remained friends and saw each other a few times during her remaining years. She died very young from cancer.

As you can see from the above account, time means nothing to the soul. The soul stands in the Magnetic Universe, above time, and when we lift our consciousness up into our souls, we can make contact with our soul mates.

My soul and your soul knows how to put our bodies in the right place at the right time. You and I have choice. We only need to *desire* someone special in our lives and to become special someones ourselves. *That is the primary way for all soul mate relationships to begin.* Your desire to bond with your opposite initiates the manifestation at physical reality levels.

You can do it! What others have done, or are doing, can be done by yourself. I can, I have, and you can. Begin your own glorious adventure now. Move your consciousness into the transcendent awareness that you are the ruler of your destiny.

Ellen Chappelle Pietsh

6

What Are You Looking For?

*Where amid the infinite sparks that light the skies of life is the one
my soul yearns and burns to know?*

We all hold an image of our most *immediate* ideal counterpart. That
male or female in human form is a source of great attraction to our
souls and minds. Every form of evolving life is governed by ideals.
These ideals give us visions of new worlds to conquer, new strength
to overcome old weaknesses, an infinite measure of new possibilities
that stretch our minds and our wills. The new ideals allow us hope
and joyful anticipation of days ahead.

A consciously growing individual moves on from one ideal to
another—that is the natural thrust of the evolution of awareness and
the form that centers that awareness. What begins in the mind of God
or human, scientist, saint, mystic, or sensitive, is an idea that is
gradually embodied into material form. The highest form of that idea
known to us is our ideal of it. The idea or vision of something more
desirable moves down from the mind into that great human
computer called a brain, carried into expression by electrical light
waves. The variety of physical forms on earth today are expressions
once held in the mind as an ideal.

As we each search for someone special in our lives, we are motivated by a picture of "perfection" already imprinted within our beings. If we are drawn to dark-haired or blond, brown-eyed or blue-eyed men or women, it is because that image comes closest *at this time* in our lives to our ideal. It may change a month or a year from now. Thus, when we start the search in earnestness for an equal to balance our lives, we would be wise to know what we are looking for. We should be able to think it through for a moment and then sit down and put it in writing. Write exactly what kind of looks, what kind of temperament, what degree of spirituality, what size, what shape, what skin tone, and whatever other specific attributes or aspects we want to see in our soul mate. Or, draw a picture, preferably in color, of that special someone. That picture is worth a thousand words. Detail it as much as possible—the shape of head, length of hair, color of eyes and so forth.

Before Pam arrived in my life in Virginia Beach, I drew an almost perfect likeness of her head, profile, and length of hair. I like shoulder length or longer hair on a woman. She arrived with shoulder length hair just as I had pictured! However, within one week she changed the "package" by cutting her hair almost to a crewcut. I was astonished and somewhat taken back when she presented her new image to me, but realized that I needed to allow her that choice. I was very glad when she let it grow back to shoulder length again!

Remember, what you unfalteringly focus on with power and determination is what you get. We will practice this creative manifesting technique by working from the known, using concrete, rather than abstract images. It is always the easiest way to envision, and subsequently manifest, that known desire through intense feeling and focus upon it. You have a blueprint to work with and like draws like.

There is another approach which is far more challenging, but infinitely more rewarding. Instead of working from structure or specifics that are known in the Electric Universe, you simply center yourself within the God of your being in the Magnetic Universe and call forth your exact equal, someone who is at that same moment what you are in consciousness, except that you want someone of the opposite sex. That person will reflect everything you are. He or she will perfectly mirror all your great strengths or weaknesses and your godly virtues. This unity is greatly rewarding. Your own divine qualities are reinforced when you see them reflected back to you. It builds up your self-worth and confidence, thus less guilt and other such worthless baggage to carry. As you love and appreciate those mirrored qualities in yourself, you are able to love and appreciate them more in others. And when you see a weakness through a soul mate reflection of that weakness, you are finally in a position to acknowledge it and become strong in that area instead. If you are ignorant, meaning you are unaware of any limitations or faults, there is no possibility of *re-form!*

I completely disagree with the concept that ignorance is bliss. Who would ever want that kind of bliss? Ignorance simply keeps you in the dark and keeps you unnecessarily limited. The only person who has transcended ignorance is someone who has ascended, but how many people have you seen ascend? Until that moment, all of us are in various degrees of ignorance, some great and perhaps for a tiny few, the amount of ignorance may be almost undetectable.

There is nothing wrong with ignorance if the ignorant one is open to new ideas. No wise individual judges the ignorance of another, for that in itself would be ignorant. Each person we meet in life is exactly as limited or unlimited as he or she desires to be in this moment! Why should anyone judge or throw stones at anyone who is doing what he or she wants to do through some divine choice? We can only allow and go on our way. Through close daily contact with an equal, the opportunity to know ourselves increases dynamically. I experience this new knowing almost every day, sometimes several times a day. An unknown equal drawn to us by our desire will bring many fresh new awarenesses in our lives.

Go into the silence of your being and think out and feel out what it is that you desire most of all in your coming mate. That is where your power and magnetism to "make it so" lies. If you already specifically know what you want, then follow all the steps outlined in the chapters ahead. When you know you are already there, it's only a matter of time. You are well on your way toward holding that specific special someone in your arms soon. If you are one of those rare individuals who simply wants a mirror or equal to come forth from the great unknown void, then focus on that! You may choose either concrete or abstract mind to manifest. *Concrete mind* is limited to the Electric Universe of known things; it moves as light waves from specific to specific. *Abstract mind* works with the Magnetic Universe, moving from the whole directly to the specific, the motion is from the general to the particular. Concrete mind takes things apart, it divides or separates the whole. Abstract mind puts things together, it unifies and synthesizes all forms in three-dimensional life expression.

If you have only a little understanding of how this duality of mind works, you can use it as the powerful creative tool that it was designed to be. Knowledge always speeds up and eases any process, while ignorance gropes blindly for desired results. In the same way that it requires effort to stay alive, while it is easy to die, it takes effort to garner wisdom, while it takes no effort to remain in the worst unconscious ignorance.

Any idea that your equal exists only at one level is entirely false. There are several major distinct sex-points, or points of contact between sexes of opposite polarity. For example: your ideal mate could have a great physique and be very good-looking, and also be extremely neurotic and unbalanced emotionally. On the other hand, that mate could have a perfectly balanced or centered consciousness, both mentally and emotionally, but possess a malformed body, or what may be considered to be coarse or even ugly features. Likewise, a physically attractive male or female may have a cold, materialistic mind, hence "a cold fish." What if an individual had a wonderfully integrated personality, an attractive body, plus warm, loving feelings, and great intelligence? Unless this description also fits you to a "T," this mate is not for you. His or her personality may differ from yours. His or her values or approach to reality may be universes, or even light years, away from yours. The diversity in our universe is wonderfully infinite and often unique. All ideals are relative to the carrier of them.

What is most important of all to evaluate is balance or alignment. Do his or her energies harmonize with yours? Or conflict? When you are in harmony or accordance with another it means he or she is flowing along the same line of force or wave of energy. Your flow is then together. Your movement is side-by-side in the same forward direction, not diagonal, counter-clock-wise, or at cross-angles to each other. These differences show clearly to a knowledgeable observer.

You will find, when you have a balanced exchange with another, that a spirit of harmony unfolds between you and that mate, friend, stranger, or loved one. When you are out of alignment or balance with another, there is disagreement, and the degree of mal-alignment or discontent soon becomes apparent.

Most of those who only attract us on the physical plane of reality are but fleeting reflections of our great ideal. That is why few of them hold any long-lasting relationships with us. For this or that fickle reason, a purely surface relationship, friendship, or love affair is known briefly and fades. What appears often at first glance to be a glittering ideal may soon turn into a greatly tarnished idol. The surface glamor wears away to show that what we thought was valuable gold or silver is only lead or zinc! Thus, our souls chalk up another failure and sad memory in our recording of life.

Over countless centuries we have all recorded memories that were shared briefly or over a lifetime with ideal mates. Most of us have had many thousands upon thousands of amorous encounters with the opposite sexes through thousands of human lifetimes. Many times, the same key lover may have appeared to share exquisite relationships with our soul. Individually, and collectively, all these greatly charged memories generate admixtures of ideals from that great grid or pool. All our past relationships still linger within us, indelibly impressed and recorded in our souls. They are there forever in our subconscious and superconscious memory banks, the inert gases of the Electrical Universe.

Our soul mate is not of the same sex as ourselves. Nowhere in nature does such a possibility exist. That great ideal is only embodied in the form of our opposite sex, thus holding an attraction for us to fuse with the whole self, whole-I, or holy self. We naturally seek to find complete at-one-ment, or oneness, with that one who is an equal mirror of our own self.

Sex is sex. It really does not matter whether sex unification occurs between a man and a woman, or between two atoms, or two solar systems. The outer sex relationship is only a reflection of the inner unity of all life. Sex movement is simply the natural effort or desire to be one-with-another! This outward reach of consciousness toward any ideal form of life, large or small, constitutes the eternal quest and active pursuit toward Greater-Self! In the thrilling act of fusion or becoming more of ourself, through any natural act of union we feel pleasure and "more-ness." To become parted, or less of self, naturally feels painful and restrictive. This natural balanced selection of an ideal exists within all dimensions and kingdoms of life. That is why birds know birds, dogs know dogs, and each seeks its mate. If birds and bees and butterflies know how to do it, so do you! Feel out what you desire and go for it!

7

Where Do You Look?

Where is the other part of me?
I look both high and low.
Where, oh, where do I go?

Our hearts cry,
where, oh, where is he or she,
This elusive soul mate of mine!
Here and there,
in the circle and square.
Answers Guardian Time!

First, to be a soul mate, your mate must be found at the soul level. Once the contact through desire is established there, you can start to anticipate outer plane or physical contact. Mind is everywhere, so at that initial point of desire, he or she is connected to you. The *intent* of time is established. The *event* of time must follow as your destiny.

We ignorantly give most of our focus to the problem, instead of focusing on the solution. As we do that, following universal law, the problem grows larger. Focus is what draws forth enhancement or enlargement of whatever is being focused on. Where, then is our focus?

Looking back upon our lives, it seems that we have searched the four corners of earth with ceaseless, timeless energy to find that

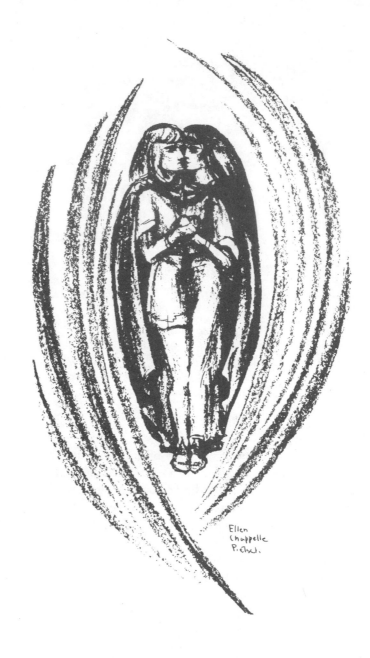

Ellen
Chappelle
P. clsch.

imagined perfect male or female mate. Where is that boy or girl, that man or woman, who is the living end to our dreams, and we to them? Most seekers have explored only the three known dimensions, or three corners of earth. Some, disappointed and dulled by their failures have given up their search. Others keep plodding on persistently at donkey-rate speed. The failures have come because of our failure to look into that fourth corner, the fourth dimension of consciousness.

It is in that fourth area where the secret source and cause of our constant yearning lies securely hidden. Meanwhile, our search has carried us through a labyrinth of trails, up and down, back and forth, across the many paths and crossroads, or highways and byways of earth. Most of those journeys have led absolutely nowhere! We have found that every newfound trail ended at the top of the first rise, or got lost on the plains of sorrow. No matter, our ever-yearning, ever-burning, seemingly hopeless search goes on. That eternally persistent question teases and taunts our minds. Does he or she really, truly exist?

Yes! He or she is waiting for you. Somewhere, there is someone who is now already perfectly intertwined with your own unique destiny. He or she is someone precious to you, someone with whom you will experience floods of rapturous joy and bliss when your desire flames strong enough to bring you together. Like attracts like. Opposites do not attract. That is an impossibility in nature, opposites only oppose!

These four corners, four points of nature, and four points of sexual contact—the physical, mental, emotional, and soul natures—blend, or multiply and divide from out of a fifth point where *spirit* presides. Thus the many references to human beings as five-pointed stars.

The three most powerful points of contact between any human entities are between spirit and spirit, soul and soul, and personality and personality, and in that order. Compatibility at either of these first two levels keeps or holds a relationship strong. Since personalities are fickle, disunity can arise and swiftly destroy what appeared to be a good relationship within moments. Conditional love finds it easy to convert into hate through ignorance. Any of the lesser three sexual contact areas—mental, emotional, or physical communication—are even more fragile bonds. Contact between twin souls is intensely powerful, but appears to occur only when that unique pair of mates are in their last human lifetime, when *ascension* occurs. This will be amplified in a later chapter.

The point being established here for you now is that each added point of sexual contact between yourself and your equal increases the balance shared, thus the joy and bliss experienced between them. It follows, that when two of these major sex points are aligned between soul mates, their union or marriage will be strong and durable. They have unified and thus doubled their feelings of more-ness through their intimate mirror of likeness. Can you imagine the sheer ecstacy that could be experienced between mates if all of these electrical and magnetic points of contact were balanced between them? It's known as heaven on earth!

It is highly unusual to find more than one (and often none) of these possible points of balance (or union) lined up between marriage "partners" during our present Age of Slaughter. This explains quite clearly why marriages without a sound basis of communication or balanced interchange fall apart quickly. If, on the other hand, they are held together in an unholy alliance, because of social demands or other worldly pressures, then that so-called marriage is a living hell on earth! Marriages must be held together because a sacred pact is made between the God of your being and the God of your marriage partner's being. All vows are sacred to the soul. That is why in all advanced civilizations, not in one so debased as ours, great caution is taken to assure selection of a marriage partner to whom one is committed for a full lifetime! The only true marriage that exists is the natural one, found in love, between any or all of the basic sex points of contact between you and your mate. Any other definition by church or state is often an insult to our intelligence. No contract on paper, containing all the words and promises in the world, will uphold what is put together in ignorance and decreed or ordained as a "holy marriage!" The marriage is holy because you and your mate have made it that. Period.

The wonderful thing about new knowledge is that it does open up new doors and new possibilities. When an educated public can become aware of these major and minor sexual meeting places between them, soul mates will know and search out only their equals, and marriages will begin to last for a lifetime once again.

Once we know what we are searching for, we will find success. Not knowing leads toward the same old, blind wandering in the dark. What is needed is intelligent direction, the clear light of knowledge to speed us on our way. What then appeared like a long torturous trail winding endlessly will be greatly shortened as we discover and apply proven techniques of manifestation to help us along our way.

Sex—merely a three-letter word—contains far more meaning than the wildest heights, breadths, and widths of our imaginations. Without sex, physical form would not exist. Our entire universe would be nonexistent! In all our vast seeming reality, only sex, or dual polarity, makes existence possible. Sex exists on every plane and dimension; there is mental sex, emotional sex, as well as a universal physical sex.

It is not unreasonable to be intelligently ordered or scientific in your already emotional search for your equal, or soul mate, especially when you know how mismatched almost all marriages are today. My own past marriages ended because of my own past ignorances. I thank God in the highest heavens and the depths of my being that I know the true sacred value of my marriage today. These new insights should enable you to see the rationale of applying careful thought as well as feeling into your search for your mate. When you know what you want, and where to go, you are bound to get it!

Look before you leap! The wonderful one before you may be marvelously compatible at physical levels, but far too cold or aloof for you at mental and emotional levels, or vice versa. You might engage with someone well at a personality level, but may be at great odds with that person at a soul purpose. A wise person uses all the knowing possible to make sure she or he calls forth and aligns self with an equal loved one. Keep both eyes wide open! Eliminate blind, wishful emotion, or action that keeps turning you around in circles.

Nevertheless, seek and you will find. However, all seeking *implies first knowing,* which equals active intelligence.

There are many as yet unconnected, untouched areas or plateaus of awareness between you and your special someone. How you discover and fill those voids with equal and balanced interchanges is your business. I know that it is possible to bridge across from one level to another if desire, character, and love of self are strong enough.

The most obvious place to find your soul mate is in the intimate field of your daily life, while at work, at study, or at play. Once your inner contact forged by your strong desire is made, all the exterior things you do act magnetically to draw your beloved one to you. That equal will inevitably hear your call and will be drawn into the net of your action as you go forward with your daily affairs. That has been my experience, as well as the experience of all those I know who are today matched with their soul mates. We found each other at the least expected moment. The meeting occurred while both of us were diligently pursuing our regular daily activity and productivity. *Action breeds action!*

While you and I are busy doing what we are doing, we stand a good chance of conjuncting with our soul mate at the appropriate crossroad, who just so happens to be doing the same thing. Through mutual activity at the same time and in the same place, a meeting, a fusion, or a cohesion between your soul mate and yourself must emerge. Physical effort made to go here and there with a driving motive to look for your soul mate is a pure waste of time! All that useless circling around actually delays your meeting.

In mystic circles there is an apt saying, "The mind is the slayer of the real." We are talking about the electrical, reflexive monkey-mind which only appears to be thinking. First, know, then go! When the physical concrete mind makes plans that take you toward searching hither and thither, you are doing what you *think*, instead of what you *know*. Instead of being where you would be according to your natural flow, you follow the artful, enticing illusions of your mind. You lead yourself here and there in hot pursuit of that place or that time where you might suddenly meet your loved one. That kind of thinking only puts you on false trails and your natural path is left behind.

When we follow concrete mind, which innately turns in circles upon itself, we lose temporary contact with our soul or knowing self. We are then lost in our senses where illusion and darkness prevail. Monkey mind does not, but spirit always knows our next best move. A sharply attuned person moves without hesitation to do what needs to be done next. The correct feeling or answer is usually always the one that comes to consciousness first. That feeling does not have a judging mind to cast doubts or fears into the picture. This only happens after the first awareness or idea arrives.

When we do what we know we desire to do, we are doing what comes naturally to us. At this same time, if our soul mate has also stopped following a busy-bee monkey-mind, and is busy doing his or her thing, then he or she will converge normally into our electrical field of awareness, or vice versa. Converging lines of motion do meet eventually.

All vertical or inner movement finds its way to the outer plane in a direct line of descent from Oneness to Oneness, spirit to spirit, soul to soul, personality to personality, mind to mind, feeling to feeling and that similar converging physical to physical environment. Bingo! If either one of these equals or soul mates gets side tracked or "misses" the connection in this natural inner to outer line of descent, they will also miss the connection or fusion with the counterpart. Free will always enters in.

While still spinning around and around in meaningless getting-no-where circles, there is little chance of alignment or contact between equal or kindred souls at physical levels. It is always the act of *being yourself* that allows your soul to take silent, calm control. It, then, is your constant and sure guiding influence. You are what you are in consciousness, and that is what your soul mate is as well. It is the qualities you two have in common that will draw you to each other, whether you are the masculine or feminine counterpart of the other.

Where must I look? How will I meet and know my soul mate? These are the most-asked questions I have encountered. They were once on my mind as well. I did not meet my "one and only" mate until I myself was consciously awake and ready for that meeting. Even then, it was unexpected.

If you do your work, you can be assured that God will do his. *He will not do it for you!* That grand encounter with your loved one only can occur when you have made a conscious decision to "quit playing the field." The moment you know, beyond any doubt or fear that you are willing to give all your love and life commitment to your divine ideal, she or he will appear in your life!

While writing this chapter, a wonderful close friend asked for my advice concerning finding his soul mate. Knowing his ways, I explained he would need to leave his vast harem of beauties behind and quit playing the field. He then admitted he loved his life of variety more than the idea of one ideal. He wanted to woo and possess his soul mate temporarily. He reminded me of "the rich young man," who, when told by Sananda 2000 years ago, "Give up your worldly possessions and follow me," turned sadly away. He loved his possessions too much to part with them and was then not worthy of entry into the kingdom of heaven.

My greatly beloved friend will not meet his soul mate as long as he keeps that attitude. He wanted a soul mate "for only a month or two" as he put it. The inner self is constant and ongoing. It is not fickle, or concerned or drawn to passing things.

An almost sure indication that your soul is beginning to have paramount influence over you is when a sudden new sense of responsibility and commitment to grander and greater ideals awakens within you. Not that my friend is soulless. He is obviously soulmateless, but he does have a great amount of pure human charm and soul force in most all other areas. At present, his alter-ego, or personality, is intentionally blocking out that soul force needed to manifest his equal in his life. When he chooses and is ready to live a life of full, joyful commitment in monogamy with his own great ideal, she will appear.

Meantime, my friend candidly admits that his ever ongoing physically engaging sexual affairs are almost totally devoid of love, during, or after, the sex act. He admits, too, that his girlfriends conveniently fulfill his carnal drives as outlets for his feelings of lust. He knows the deeper, divine soul-fulfilling feelings he craves are missing in his relationships. Observedly, at this time in his life, he prefers to feed on, or hold onto, his flesh and bones possessions at the great expense of an aching spiritual hunger that continues to remain unfed.

Ask yourself now, are you truly ready for your soul mate? Be sure to give yourself a truthful reply! Are you the kind of person you would like to meet coming out of a door toward you now? Are you somone that your beloved counterpart will instantly love and respect? If not, why not? Your unreadyness for an equal, or your inability to love yourself will keep the door tightly shut between you and the one you want to meet at a soul level. This door can only be unlocked from the inside by yourself!

In reality, your soul mate is a helpmate of the opposite sex who can help *you* bring balance and fulfillment to yourself. She or he is a perfect mirror. Your other relationships will eventually fall away. Only that divine human bond found at soul level holds and endures through sickness and health, prosperity and adversity. That is a real marriage!

To reiterate, the fourth dimension holds the key to our search for a soul mate. Physical mates meet at a physical level. Emotional mates meet at an emotional level, but soul mates meet and merge with each other as ecstatic, creative, evolving, and living souls. How could you or anyone else expect to find your soul mate at a lesser degree of life? Only your loftiest thoughts, feelings, and living actions can touch and move the soul of an equal to reciprocal, balanced response. May you lift up and touch those pinnacle heights within you now, for that is where your beloved one will appear!

Ellen Chappelle Pietsch

8

The Law of Magnetic Attraction

Under heavens high,
or mid waters deep,
burning with the fire of desire,
come, come to me.

The Magnetic Universe is the cause of all dual effects we see and experience in our three-dimensional Electric Universe. Your soul mate is attracted to you because you both radiate the same magnetic qualities. Like always seeks like, otherwise a handful of sand could never accumulate together. The one who is like you is naturally attracted to you, and vice versa. This attractive force will lead your soul mate to you, or lead you to this person, at some point and time in space, just like the grains of sand found their affinity together.

The very nature of consciousness provides an inner link between ourselves and past or present other selves related to us. Every day, more and more people are beginning to realize that thoughts are alive with power. We literally create every environment that our onlooking consciousness perceives before us. There is a mighty tremendous potency in every thought we focus upon in our force field or aura. We eventually become what we think and do. Our soul force, or spirit, the source of our thoughts, has infinite power to transform our living conditions from better to better, or for worse. One thought alone is powerful enough to change the chemistry of our physical bodies from alkaline to acid and bring on a deathly illness. That power has always been innate and almost totally unknown or ignored by us. It's time to wake up!

In a previous chapter, I revealed my own personal experiences with Bonnie when the force of my soul actually took me bodily into juxtaposition with certain outer plane events that had been pre-ordained and previsioned by my conscious mind ten years before that event. My physical body was controlled and put in the exact place, at the exact time, so that I would meet the destiny of that very startling experience, as was predicted to my mind by my soul a full decade prior!

Our souls are all-powerful when it comes to controlling any division of the three-fold personality. Your own powerful mind stands behind and with that soul of yours. When you are certain within your soul that you are eagerly ready to meet physically with your soul mate, then somewhere, somehow, sometime on the physical plane you will do it. If he or she is not yet quite ready to make an outer physical connection with you, your blazing and focused determination could help speed up the process. The fire of mind actually burns away all the existing hindrances between you and your loved ones.

Coupled with the mind, there is nothing in this world as strong and potent as emotional desire, fed by the flame of higher love and inspiration. When your whole being yearns and burns to be with that equal one who waits eagerly for you, your chance of that glorious meeting gains unlimited power. Like my beloved friend, it means you, too, must take your mind off the many in the marketplace and focus on the one. Can you do it? If you can, the law will go to work for you and your soul mate will be attracted into your living presence.

Every atom and particle, every large or small point of con-sciousness is governed by law. We have learned about some of these laws in school. Human beings have formulated or made certain laws into formulas. They govern our lives—though limited and some-times unjust; they govern physics, chemistry, mathematics, optics, and other structure, or form sciences—though many are false.

Since all things must have a source of "entry" into physical existence, where do these laws come from? They all emerge into our consciousness by way of mind, beginning as ideas. If formulated correctly, then these laws are established under the appropriate category. They are laws because they can be proved endlessly to produce the same results under the same actions. Many human minds have teamed up to produce each one of these vast overcomplex so-called laws of science today. But these laws are based on the illusions of the senses and have kept people ignorant over the ages.

On the other hand, a few searching minds discovered some specific, accurate, and immutable laws of Nature, relating to the smallest particle or largest universe. On other planets, billions of years ago, these laws had already been known and carried to human-bearing planets like our Earth. The science transcended form, though by nature it included all structure. These life scientists, mystics, saints, sages, or seers made every effort to inform the masses about these laws. They have often been referred to as the mysteries, or the science of life. The law of the Magnetic Universe is the major specific universal law of life. It is your knowledge and use of these laws that enable you, or any other man and woman, to consciously focus and draw a soul mate to yourself or you to them. In the Magnetic Universe only oneness exists. All points in space are simultaneous![3]

Supposedly, according to current theories, opposites are attracted to each other; that is why they say a female is attracted to a male and vice versa. No. Emphatically, no. Opposites only oppose. However, likes are always attracted to likes. We like those who think and feel as we think and feel and are repulsed by those who do not. "Birds of a feather flock together." The old axiom covers this aspect

---

[3] For readers interested in reading more about these theories, the author refers them to the Pleiadian Documents, published by America West Publishers, PO Box 986, Tehachapi, CA 93581. As far as the author is concerned, they contain the greatest pool of scientific knowledge assembled on Earth. Titled *The Pleiades Connection*, the work contains eight volumes. Write for a price list. You can also ask for a free sample of their newsletter, The Phoenix Liberator, published weekly.

of the law of attraction nicely. Your soul mate is like you. He or she has a certain tone, chord, or note that strikes the same key in your consciousness.

Where is he or she at this moment? A mere thought away! He or she is also searching for the ways or means to be with you. It will be the work of the law of magnetic attraction that will speed up that electric moment when you look into each other's eyes and joyously plumb the depths of each other's soul, knowing, recognizing, and exalting in the fact that the two of you are finally together as one.

Never underestimate the great value of *knowing* and then working with powerful laws of nature. Each of these laws is continuous and unchangeable. One law can be used to bolster or offset another. The law of gravity has held us bound to earth for some time, yet by knowing and using the law of aerodynamics, we now soar through the air faster than any high flying bird. That grand law of aerodynamics has always been there in nature waiting patiently for us to become aware and make use of it, forever a part of the science of life. Yet, only when it was known and brought forth into three-dimensional existence by mind and gathered into a specific formula, in the form science of which it is a part, and then used, that planes, rockets, spaceships, and other airborne vehicles were produced.

These powerful laws have always existed. Our secret inner world government not only knows them but is using them to control our lives. Laws can be used for construction or destruction. The life of all humanity is put into jeopardy at this moment through their misuse.

Knowledge of certain laws can be brought into play to speed up your physical meeting with your soul mate. The following important and very basic law can be used by anyone: *energy follows thought*. All energy springs from the Magnetic Universe via thought. Energy assures the growth of yourself or of an idea. No energy equals death.

If you desire to attract your soul mate, the process can be compared to being lost in a wilderness and building a fire to attract the attention of other humans. The more fuel or energy you add to the fire, the bigger the blaze and smoke gets until it can be seen for miles and will hopefully attract another pair of human eyes to your plight. By the same process, as you build the fire of desire bigger and bigger in your mind and soul, the more chance it will attract the object of your desire, as your desire becomes radiantly intensified. There is a direct ratio between the speed at which any idea or desire becomes concrete and the intensity within it!

The electrical pressure of being hot or cold makes you attractive or repulsive. These attitudes or polarities are equally effective in drawing someone to you or in driving them further away. Time or distance does not matter, since the Magnetic Universe posture nullifies both time and space. If you do not care whether or not your soul mate appears, then the very coolness of your attitude keeps him or her repulsed and at a safe distance from you and your signal. On the other hand, by giving energy to the idea of being with a special someone who is your equal, you actually create a living pathway of consciousness between yourself and that unique human soul who appeals so much to your tastes in male or female essence! It is important to know that energy follows thought. Now you may knowingly speed up what you desire. It's simple. The technique is to give more concentrated thought, thus more focused desire or energetic feeling to your want.

Once you intensify or focus your energy toward your soul mate, the law of Magnetic Attraction begins immediately to work with you to make your dream a reality. It does not matter where on earth your loved one lives. He or she will automatically react and respond to your new state of consciousness and will progress physically toward you. You have opened the door between your loved one and yourself, and one joyous day he or she will walk through it into your life. An open door in consciousness opens equivalent doors three-dimensionally.

Another pertinent law of the Science of Life is *form must conform to consciousness.* That is why terms we hear about such as "poverty consciousness" or "prosperity consciousness" are very valid. Whichever of these two opposites you or I dwell in during the majority of our waking hours faithfully reproduces that state at a physical level in your life and mine. Form must conform to consciousness. It is the law!

The most important question for you now is do you really want to be with a soul mate as soon as possible? If your answer is yes, then make your desire a reality within the time frame chosen by yourself. It's your time; it's your choice. Instead of being fated and bound by existing limited patterns, you change the future to be what is chosen and thus destined by your own divine intervention!

The law works when you work it. If you wish to experience your soul mate at more than just a mental, emotional, or physical level, you must specify your objective clearly. Then your concentrated focus establishes a physical result. Otherwise, your desire remains on the mental plane and works out only in your daydreams or dreams while asleep. The starting point for a glorious full-bodied physical result is in you. All the how-to-do-it methods are outlined in this volume. Exactly what kind of a man or woman are you looking for? What are you doing about it? Put it down in writing now. Do you have better things to do? I wish you God-speed on your adventurous way!

9

Preparing a Receptive Self-Image

Where is my other me?
I keep looking so.
Where did I go?

Depending on the state of your present self-image, this may be the most important chapter in this book. The image you hold of yourself determines your success or failure in everything. Ponder it for a moment. What do you really think about yourself? *Do you like you?* Are you able to think of yourself as one who succeeds in all or most objectives, or does the idea that you can't do it dominate your conscious thoughts? Each woman or man who succeeds in bringing a soul mate into her or his life is an individual with a good self-image. That kind of person is also a doer. She or he is an "actualizer," a person who makes desires come true by acting on them.

If you have accepted an idea of inferiority concerning your looks, your talents, or your ability to make and keep friends or be successful, then you better stop and re-think your position. Be assured, in many ways you are quite extraordinary. You are different. There is no other single being in the universe exactly like yourself. You innately have talents and new approaches to reality that no one else can match!

Ellen Chobbelle Pietsch

Know that every soul in human form is divine. Some human souls display the radiance of their identity and divinity more clearly than others; it is their time and their season. Yours is only a thought and an action away!

It is an infinite truism—you have no limitations except the ones you have accepted and thus imposed upon yourself. That same truth applies to myself and all other human beings anywhere in any universe. Your beliefs help to create every seeming reality you experience. There are no exceptions. This is again one of the universal laws of nature at constant work within all of you.

Do you really know what beliefs you hold hidden within you? Very few in human form do! Once we examine and discard the false beliefs we hold about ourselves and the seeming reality around us, the sooner our limitations will disappear. The truth does make us free!

Face and forget what you have for so long falsely believed. Hopefully, one day very soon, you will know you can tap and use the power of the whole universe to make your dreams come true. All knowledge and power is freely available to every single fragmented Self of the SELF. God moves in you now! It is only through God that you live and move and have your being. The earth and all other worlds can come and go ten trillion times, but you will always be! You are at your center more than any part of the reality, you are *all* of it. You are supreme over all things. You can take your place at your center and shape and recreate worlds, so why do you accept any belief that allows you less?

The power of a single thought is immense. Your belief is strong enough to make your worlds appear or disappear! The sad part is any false belief of limitation also does precisely that. It limits you, the holder of that thought.

In a limited three-dimensional reality, a false belief is just as powerful as a true belief. However, the instant you stop giving your power—meaning your life energy or focus—to a false belief, it ceases to hold any power over you or over your worldly affairs. Energy follows thought, so what you give life to lives within you and your world. On the other hand, what you cease to give life to must die out of your conscious reality and world.

Every single human being in this majestic universe has been given the unique gift of free choice. What an incredibly divine gift, for it thereby makes us equal co-creators with God. Because of free choice, we each live in the kind of world we have chosen to live in. It is solely my belief or knowingness that produces my thoughts and their appropriate limited or unlimited feelings, my limited or unlimited and self-created physical body, and my limited or unlimited self-created physical world that I find myself in. The same statement applies to yourself. Your create your attitude, your body, your world, for good or for not-so-good, or worse.

Why do beliefs have so much power? Because they stem from ideas and thoughts which are the primary origin of every reality we are able to know and experience. A belief affixes itself into three-dimensional reality from either end of its duality. One end, or one face, is polarized into faith or knowingness, and the other face within this pair of opposites is the face of fear or doubt! Either one of these two equally strong electric states of consciousness is able to move and change your world. Fear is equally powerful to faith. Either state brings equivalent construction or destruction.

Remember, energy follows thought. Take care of what you fear, for your fear may bring itself into your reality! Knowing this, doesn't it behoove us to stop giving our precious life energy to ancient habits of supporting foolish fears?

God gifted us with priceless free choice. When you know the difference between the two faces of faith and fear, would you choose to remain fearful? Our focus deserves to be on an open mind, not a closed one, on productive good thoughts and feelings, not on self-destructive and annoying or nagging fears and doubts.

Stop warring with yourself! Peace does not come from hating war. That only adds more hatred into life. Peace comes from loving peace. Stand up before the awesome mirror of your consciousness. Decree that you are not weak! You are not inferior! You are not inadequate! All these false beliefs must be left behind. Give them no more energy by denial either. Simply know these have been false assumptions held about yourself in the past. These negative experiences belong only to the past. You now know better. Let them serve only as valuable lessons. Don't carry any regrets about what you have done in past ignorance and innocence. The lesson was *don't do it again!* Give thanks that you are wiser now, instead.

If you strongly believe you are a loser, or a weak and inferior person, or inadequate in any way, your right-down-to-earth experiences will mirror it. You have learned, or are learning now through experience, that your beliefs—true or false—have great power. Why then not make a pact with yourself now? Question every single old belief you ever held or are holding now, as well as all of these new ones coming your way. If you do this, using your own God-given reason as the guidepost, you will master and control your world. You will be the arbiter, the ruler of your destiny!

Remember, your mind is a container. Garbage in, garbage out! Get rid of the old garbage and refuse to allow any more old garbage that limits you in any way. Your self-image is highly important. If you truly love yourself first, then you will also be able to love others. If you distrust yourself, you will distrust others. What a choice! You experience what you give to life.

There is one last pertinent universal law concerning our current theme of self-image. You get what you give! The converse is also law. You lose what you hold! Think this through. If these laws are true, and I know they are, would it not be wise to give yourself the very best, instead of the worst in life? Why *debit* yourself, when you can just as easily *credit* yourself with sublime love, unlimited wealth, superb health, a zestful vitality, and on-going self-success?

Remember, there is always some kind of "time lag" between a thought and the precipitation of that idea materially. So for a time look beyond the world of seeming appearance. The law always prevails, form must conform to consciousness. In due time, the old and now undesirable state of your false being will disappear. The differently knowing and focused *new you* will stand tall, triumphant, and victorious over all! Your newly accepted self-image now allows you to be an awakening god-woman or god-man on earth! I would say that giving thanks would be appropriate.

10

Visualization Techniques

Which me in you will you unveil
to make my earthly dream come true?

Every wise teacher involved with training individuals to achieve success in life will make his or her students aware of the vital part that visualization plays in making a goal become a reality. A picture is worth more than a thousand words! Visualization means we use thoughtful imagination, that fantastic image-making faculty of our minds, to create something new in our lives. Through the art of visualization, we stretch our consciousness beyond the limits of time-present. We look forth and see the end from the beginning. We hold a clear mental picture of the end results we desire. We never waver from that focus for a moment. When so doing, we are able to arrive at a point in the future to find that our imagined picture has turned into a full-bloom reality!

The power of your mind, or any mind, is so incredible that it defies belief. What we can imagine, we can make an experienced reality. Napoleon Hill popularized this exact same idea when he coined the phrase, "What we can conceive and believe, we can achieve!"

In the past I have traveled extensively and have given many lectures on how to make dreams come true. In one instance I told my audience in a small church in Tampa, Florida, how a man and his wife had created a two-story apartment complex without spending a penny.

Among my audience was an extremely destitute family, a mother and five children, to whom I allowed free attendance. I explained to my fairly large weekend audience that I had also taken myself out of abject poverty through the same visualization techniques. Within six months, starting from zero, I owned a home of my own, a Cadillac, and had a far about average monthly income. That hard-pressed mother and her children listened with an open mind and a unified resolve to do the same thing. At one of the breaks in my talk, the mother took me aside and said she and her children were going to manifest a home for themselves within one week! I marvelled at their faith, but I did not throw cold water on their resolve. Instead, I agreed, that if all of them were totally united in that belief they would do it.

One week later I sat on the bare floor of their new home. A spaghetti dinner had been prepared in my honor by the oldest daughter. This was their way to thank me for showing them and inspiring them so they could make their own sweet dream come true. They had no furniture, and we sat on the floor with our dishes in our laps or on the floor between our knees. They already owned the home and land, "lock, stock and barrel." The house was identical to the one they all agreed upon a week before. Through one snowballing sequence of strange but meaningful events, the house and land were generously gifted to them, no strings attached! The deed was made out jointly in the name of the mother and oldest son, who was 17.

I remembered during my seminar the youngest member of the family, who was only 7, asked more questions than anyone. This simple family listened, questioned, and humbly accepted and used the basic principles of visualization and manifestation revealed to them. The point here is that *they put their newfound knowledge into immediate practice!* This is where this extraordinary family differed greatly from the average individual or group. Instead of putting their new knowingness on the shelf, they applied it to life. They demonstrated that knowing and doing are two different things!

Many of us know, but how many of us do? How many people today are *being* their knowledge—meaning, living it? Only a handful. However, a little knowledge goes a long way, for knowledge is power, but only when used.

A Visualization Practice

1) Turn your focus within and form the clearest possible physical image you can of that special someone who is ideal for you. See clearly the color of eyes, the color of hair, the size, shape, personality traits, and anything else you can think or know is an important quality or essence in your soul mate. Make him or her the best you can imagine. Do not compromise. You will only be truly satisfied with someone who fills your order. Do not hesitate to see the most in this person. It is a fact that if you can image this person, he or she does exist! Do not ever feel you are demanding too much from the one you love. After all, he or she is your equal!

2) Think lovingly and endearingly toward this person for five to ten minutes daily, at the same regular time if possible. Then turn your attention away and go back to your daily responsibilities. Here is where many individuals fail. It is imperative that you cut the cord between yourself and the thoughtform you have sent out into the universe. Otherwise, it simply stays spiralling around in your mental body and becomes an *idée-fixe* that possesses you, or an obsession. When a child is born, the umbilical cord attached to the mother is cut. The child then goes forth to create what is in its being. So be sure you do the same thing with your thought-child. This allows it to go out into the world and make contact with that soul who is the exact counterpart of that thoughtform. Just know that a person such as you have imagined exists. It is so. Otherwise, you would never have been able to conjure or conceive those specific, unique characteristics that compose your soul mate.

3) Tell this beloved one mentally, during your five to ten minute "broadcast": your name, the town or city and country you are living

in, and anything else pertinent that you wish him or her to know about you. This thought, once aimed to your soul mate, will proceed telepathically and be "picked up" at some level or degree by him or her. Know *it is so* as you think to him or her.

4) Tell your soul mate the month, week, day, or year that you are expecting him or her to arrive physically into your life.

5) See yourself in vivid association with this soul mate in every way you can conceive of *in living color!* See yourself introducing him or her to your parents or friends. See yourself seated beside and dining with your soul mate at your favorite restaurant, or going for a long romantic walk, side-by-side in a park or in the country. See yourself working happily together on a business project, or a favorite dream yet unfulfilled. Put all the emotional zeal and colorful imagery you can muster into these soon-to-be-physical picture-association realities.

6) End each session engaged in communion with him or her giving thanks. Affirm that what you mentally envision is already a reality on the inner planes. It is only a matter of time and this person will be a manifested physical reality, as well.

7) God is the source of all gifts. Tell God how you personally will re-give this loving gift to another. This can easily be accomplished simply by sharing with another these powerful truths you have used to precipitate your own beguiling and enchanting "special some-one" into your life.

• • •

Carefully follow these visualization methods daily and you will soon achieve the desired results you are envisioning. Be sure you do not insult your own sense of credibility. If you think or feel it is impossible for this person to appear in your life in the next hour, or the next day, do not waste your time with that idea. That would put a huge hindrance in your way. Take the time to feel it out. You will sense what is the most believable time schedule to you. Then decide on what is credible, decree it to be and go forward into the hall of time with complete trust in that choice. Know that he or she will be there at the appointed or chosen time.

The great bonus is that this same technique works for anything else you want to create. Make sure that what you desire is a blessing to yourself and all affected by your desire. Do not focus on getting something from any one specific person, institution, or group. That is a mis-use of this power and violates the law of love. The penalty is great suffering and pain in the long run, because it is an act of taking without any thought of giving. When, for example, you are in need of one hundred dollars, if you envision a specific person handing you that money, it is a violation of law. The correct way requires the same kind of effort and the same amount of it. Simply ask, and focus on seeing it in *your* hands and coming from any infinite possibility in the universe. The universal supply is without end, stored in abundance with whatever you can envision. You will be inspired toward the right action.

When you know you are a divine daughter or son of God, you are immediately granted use of all the riches and power in the universe. There is more than enough to fulfill the highest dreams of every human being in Creation. What or whom you desire will come out of the great endless reservoir of life eternal. It is limitless and beyond all time.

You have just as much right to be healthy, wealthy, powerful, and successful as anyone else on Earth. Only you, though, can decide through choice how rich or poor you will be in anything. God withholds nothing from his children. "Ask and it shall be given." May what you ask for be a genuine blessing for you and all involved.

A last and most important point everyone here on earth should know is the following: when you cultivate your consciousness to be a giver, you are in the balanced flow of life. What you give will be re-given to you with interest!

When you cultivate your consciousness to be a taker, you are in total opposition to the law of love and balance. What you take will be taken from you. In this light, ask yourself the question and weigh the answer for accuracy. Looking truthfully into your conscious being, are you a giver or a taker?

The law of love is simple. What God gives must be re-given to another. What are you willing to give for whatever you are gifted with? This law of equal re-giving makes the world turn around. Be sure you know and understand this law and practice *equal and balanced* interactions with your soul mate, for then your relationship will be an enduring one.

May the soul mate you desire arrive in your life soon! May you gift him or her with your own great joy, and may he or she re-give it to you! I am, for I choose to be, your beloved friend. So be it!

11

The Power of Self-Suggestion

He or she lives deep in your memory.
When you awake,
The knowing dawn will break.

The most powerful tool any human here on Earth possesses is the simple act of self-suggestion. Whether we like it or not, our subconscious is far more powerful than our conscious mind. The only power greater is our superconscious mind, which is transcendent to physical mass. Until we have switched our conscious focus from limited self-identity and know we are wholly united with God, the next best tool to speed our evolution forward is through utilizing our subconscious. This means that instead of being mastered and ruled by our vast subconscious being, the tables should be totally turned. It must become our powerful servant while our minds become its commanding master. It is time we wisely used it, rather than being used by it—especially since that's the correct role for it to play, subservient to us, not us to it!

There is a great deal of misinformation and often fear about using this suggestive power. It is intentional, for those who manipulate and control your lives, and the lives of everyone else on Earth, through conformity to so-called "normal" social consciousness patterns use confusion to do it. If you do not know what or who to believe, then you are effectively neutralized and simply go on with the programmed pattern.

The *brain* does not think. It is simply a mechanical, physical level computer and is able to process only what is put into it. At another quantum leap, or level, "above" it, your *soul* does not think. It, too, is an inert gas chemically, and only registers or records every experience encountered eternally. Like the brain, your soul has been created to serve your human conscious mind to make choices that lead you to that chosen experience. From birth, and before, your programming began and goes on. Your soul, or subconscious, records all the experience formerly chosen by you through all your former human life expressions. While in the womb, all the thoughts, feelings, and experiences that the parents and environment provide are transmitted to it.

After birth, the programming continues, moment to moment, as weak and strong emotional data is recorded faithfully. It is literally the software that determines the limits of what you are able to process in the three-dimensional world. As the days, weeks, months, and years pass through you, almost all of these very live programs are consciously forgotten; however, the potency of their ability to rule your life is undiminished. An awakened program—through association—can stand up in your conscious mind and insist that "you can't," and this is based on childhood or ancient programming. It is always the job of the soul to bring forth your choices, your desires or wants, good or bad, since it cannot judge. It never differentiates, nor does it comprehend a non-motion as innate within the command "don't be ignorant." It can only make use of and record the last two words of that command, which tell you then "be ignorant." That is why you need to understand yourself, why and what your God-self is at every level of your fragile human expression. Ignorance breeds ignorance; wisdom breeds wisdom.

If you ponder the vast significance of this information, you will understand that wise students of life utilize this powerful self-suggestion technique to uplift and direct their life expressions. Through self-suggestion, the great reservoir of energy you command for self use is unlimited! Think about it for a moment. When a hard-working coal miner shovels fifty tons of coal from the ground into carriers provided, where does that energy come from? Certainly not from the body! It comes from the mind, which is the source of all energy, expressed through desire. If you calculate the amount of food eaten by that laboring coal miner and change it into energy units, a bare fifty pounds of lifting could be exerted. The energy to lift fifty tons from the ground into the air comes totally from the mind of the worker who believes he can shovel that much coal per day. What a wonderful miracle completely unacknowledged by our scientific community! It is inexplicable by our empirical sciences. The recording senses are the greatest deceivers we all have, because our senses only see half the motion. The equal and opposite simultaneous motion *going backward in time* is not consciously registered. If it were, then motion would be completely neutralized in a *zero universe* position. There could not then be movement, only the eternal stillness or silence out of which unending motion and sound waves seemingly appear to form ordered pictures of reality.

In the great oneness of all being, your soul has ready access to all knowledge, power, and presence. You are not limited to just your own experiences when you use your mind to connect with anything, anywhere you imagine. This is why you can use self-suggestion at appropriately known times to bring your soul mate into your life. At the same time, this immense powerhouse of your own is now controlling you, like it is doing with almost everyone else, and it can be brought sharply under control. Would you ride a horse without having a way to control its direction? Of course not! Yet, the subconscious is a million times more powerful and uncontrolled than any runaway horse. By far the best explanation of how and why this incredible subconscious mind works is detailed in the book, *The Pleiades Connection*, Volume 5[4].

Meanwhile, the most effective self-suggestions are made when your conscious mind is lulled or set aside. Then when your new "program" is entered with a great deal of desire and accompanied high emotion, you will have taken control of your destiny. You have

---

[4] See footnote 3 in Chapter 8 for more information on this eight-volume work.

given the command, and if not previously blocked by the subconscious, your desire will be fulfilled. You will be "prompted" to say, do, think, or know certain things aimed to consummate that goal.

What if your subconscious mind has already embraced a strong false belief or limitation concerning your new desire? In that case, it is necessary to track your thoughts and feelings back to the origin of the belief so strongly rooted in the shade of your subconscious. Once you know why you ignorantly accepted a limiting belief, or gave your power of self-conviction away to another outside authority, or simply deluded yourself about it, that unknown stumbling block has no further power over you. In fact, it will be as if a great load has been psychologically lifted from your shoulders. Then you merely tell yourself the truth of the situation and are free to go on your unlimited way again. If you remember that all human limitations have been accepted or self-imposed by human beings alone, then you will no longer tolerate limitations. Why? When the whole world is yours just because you desire it and follow through with God-given inspired action. Accept the genuine dignity of what and who you are. Walk tall, knowing that you are in full partnership with the greatest and most powerful partner in the universe—God Almighty in person! In this Age of Character unfolding now, anything less is really beneath your dignity. Make use of self-suggestion. It is your own divine open door to all that is!

12

Only True Prayer Works

See what the middle eye, sparked by a flaming heart,
may soon reveal.

Why are some prayers seemingly answered and others not? Is there an art to prayer? Indeed there is! Prayer is not the movement of empty lips and tireless supplications to God. Nor does it matter if you shout in the mightiest voice to God and wave your hands or shake your fists. God is never "out there," so why bother to act as if that were so. *God is within yourself and myself.* Neither is God a he or a she! God is sexless, beyond duality!

Two thousand years ago, when that great christed entity, later identified as Jesus, said, "The Kingdom of Heaven is within," he meant exactly that. The habit of looking outside ourselves for God has kept The Almighty One well hidden from sight. God can be seen in the face of every flower, in the light of every eye. All That Is stands *centered within* every person, place, or thing, within the intent of time, or the event of time. Everywhere you look, and feel, and see, our almighty God resides. God is every particle of what you are and I am. Why pretend that calling out to the high heavens or the passing wind will get an answer to your own prayer? It won't.

A great example of prayer is given in *The Pleiadian Documents.* A farmer that sows his seed in good ground after the frost of Spring

performs the first act of true prayer. God created the human being as a co-creating extension of SELF. God will work with you but not for you! The prayerful act of the farmer was on its way to fulfillment. God, in the form of nature, received the prayer and began immediately to grow the seed so that an abundant supply of corn was harvested. If, instead, the farmer had done nothing except mouth words begging God to bring in a huge harvest, that so-called prayer would have produced no harvest.

God is never more than a breath away and always more than willing to give us all we can stand to possess at any given time. Through silent communion within, all desires are known and granted immediately. However, God will not do the actual labor or act as a messenger for anyone! That is why he sent you and me into a *seemingly* three-dimensional reality to express and experience whatever idea God or co-creator man desired to manifest on Earth. You are his mind, his hands and his feet. So am I, and so is every other person, place, or thing. Through God, all seeming space and time can be collapsed. All things are thus possible.

Identity with God is paramount. When you know that you and God are ONE MIND, ONE BODY, and ONE PURPOSE, absolutely nothing can prevent you having whatever you desire. Like the wise farmer, you will know that it is only your job to get into action and plant the seed of your desire in fertile ground at the proper time and place. A seed planted by the farmer on a rock will not be able to root itself and grow. A seed planted before the frost leaves the ground will freeze and rot. Only the seed planted wisely produces an abundant harvest. God does the rest. However, if the farmer does not tend the young seedling, eliminating weeds that would choke it—like doubt that chokes fragile beliefs—the seedling may not mature properly. God sends sunshine and rain equally to all seedlings in the field. As the "hand and feet" of God, as well as the "eye" of God, it is up to you to note when your seedling (or growing idea) needs more water or shade, as your idea may need more energy or a slacking off from the intensity. Too much energy can shatter and literally electrocute it, which means death of the idea three-dimensionally.

The art of true prayer means that you focus in on whatever choice made in any given moment and give it your full attention. *Then listen for the voice within for further instruction.* As soon as you know the next step, act on it without hesitation. Do not let "monkey-mind" argue you out of your wisdom. With God, nothing is impossible, so "I can't," or "It's impossible," have no existence in God reality. God hears and knows your every thought. The ritual of speaking to God aloud verbally is only that, an empty ritual. Before your desire is expressed it is already fulfilled within. It is now merely a time-lag, and you are presiding as a midwife over the birth of the event in time. The *intent* of time was the *seed* of your desire. The *event* in time was the *birth* of your desire into the material world.

The truth that God will grant you anything and everything, but will not do it for you, must be implanted indelibly on your mind. It all begins with a desire or prayer. It ends right there if the missing link of your action is not there. The more intense your prayer or desire, the more power provided to speed it into worldly form.

The wisest prayer of all is the prayer called forth by Jesus 2000 years ago: *Lord, open me up to know all things.* What you believe is not absolute. Even what you think all day long is not absolute. Those movements of being belong to the illusionary electrical universe. However, what you know absolutely is absolute! Nothing can stand in the way of that kind of prayer.

Another important aspect of prayer explained in detail in *The Pleiadian Documents* is that our God of love gave a portion of Self to us that we might live with him in the Electrical Universe. That simple act of love is literally what makes the world turn around. What is given must be re-given to another is an eternal universal law. Without balance between, duality could not exist. Therefore, it is important to follow this law if we expect balance in our love relationships, or with our family, with our loved ones, friends, and neighbors, known or presently unknown. Any imbalance between lovers eventually destroys the relationship. The same applies to friendships and business deals. Buyer and seller must have a balanced interchange or it creates disharmony between them. This law of balance is inviolate through every intent and event of time.

Therefore, when you pray to your God within, desiring something, it is very important that you know *exactly what you are willing to re-give* to the world for that loving gift from God. The universe does not stop turning in you. To keep on turning, you must give back to the world what you have been given. In this way each small or great form of life can gift themselves with whatever measure, small or large, of life abundant they desire. As you can see, there is more than enough for everyone! You alone determine the size and the results of your prayer.

I pray the gift of this knowledge will be re-gifted to someone else from your own abundance. So be it.

Ellen
Chappelle
Pietsch

13

A Heaven-on-Earth Marriage

Soaring through celestial heights of infinite being.
We are one spirit with wings.

We do not arrive into physical birth as small babies empty-handed. Each of us possesses countless developed abilities, or capacities, and an infinite supply of yet undeveloped talents. We have earned and formed these over the long ages in the evolutionary fires of our unnumbered human experiences.

A Heaven-on-Earth marriage is formed by way of the same fragment by fragment formation. Two souls who now enjoy the splendor and joy of a soul mate union have earned it! Each in some small or large degree is living like God on Earth, leaving the petty traits and meaningless personality identities behind them. Two major changes have occurred within each of these. The personality focus has waned, and soul identity has waxed. They are soul-infused personalities, meaning that, to some degree, they master or use the marvelous personality vehicle rather than being used by it! Their electric sensations and instincts have been greatly dominated. Their love for one another is unconditional. It transcends the little petty things in life. It ignores the many small failings, even the large ones that the balanced equal mate exhibits. They now acknowledge the longtime grandeur within themselves and within their greatly beloved mirrors. There is no longer a focus on little idiosyncrasies in any other human being they used to find so disturbing within them! They do not get lost in past or future living, but live indeed within the all-encompassing immediacy of the moment, the eternal now. They are both beautiful and responsive and responsible creatures of light and character that will grow more within through the ages. They have left the Age of Slaughter behind and live grandly in the Age of Character.

Contrast this splendor to a life spent sorrowfully with a fearful, faithless, selfish ego-centered partner in an unholy marriage alliance. If this shoe fits, wear it. Then grow wisely out of it. Our states or estates of life are determined by our states of mind. Faith or fear play a big hand in them. They bring forth the positive or negative experiences we encounter. If you experience fears, doubts, and disharmony, it is not your marriage partner who constitutes your problem. It is your own ignorant feelings, prompted by false beliefs and wrong thinking. This is what gives you that irritable inner mood and highly explosive emotional temperament. You are the one pressing the panic button. If you don't like it, change it! *Face it, trace it, and erase it!* It is your own internal problem. Why hold on to it? When you let go of problems, they let go of you. They can't live without energy.

No problem is created by any person or event outside of yourself, no matter how it appears on the surface. Spare "the victim" consciousness. It's not someone else that needs an attitude change. It's yours that needs a good housecleaning. Your soul mate deserves better! But so do you!

If you want to experience a heaven on Earth marriage, it will not form overnight. Both of you will need to work on it daily. It's wise to check your own emotional temperature daily. Examine the conscious thoughts you harbor. If they are filled with irritation, you are operating at a personality level. Depression comes from too great a focus on self or on what others think about you. *What someone else thinks about you is none of your business.* They are responsible for their thoughts and actions, and you are responsible for yours. For many years now I have not been depressed or insecure, no matter how many trying and seemingly impossible hurdles are in my way. I have learned that I am not my body, or my feelings, or my mind. *I am the eternal life within and these are my instruments or servants!* Take command of your body senses. That is the first and best thing you can do for yourself. Your marriage relationship and all other interactions will be more balanced and smooth flowing.

Is married life between soul mates a constant heavenly state of bliss? Of course not! Do soul mates enjoy the mundane or simple expressions of life together? More than usual. Is there a special aura or divine protection that keeps them out of life's problems, its troubles, and its griefs? Yes, and no.

Contact with each other at the level of the soul helps uplift soul mates during trying physical, emotional, or mental times. Free choice concerning reaction is inviolate. Soul mates, like all other humans, find many things in life pleasurable. We seek to experience all the good things life offers at all levels of our beings. As a rule, when we are balanced, temperance is the keynote. Passion or ecstasy stems from greater and greater conscious union with each other and God within.

Remember, it is the daily, moment-to-moment engagement of life and the conscious overcoming that produces evolutionary growth. It takes bumping into before impact or experience is registered in our awareness. Soul mates seek to experience mutual growth, thus providing excellent mirrors in that process. They know that all progress is made through collision of their emotions (or feelings of love and hate), and their immediately reflected reactions to pleasure or pain. Some may argue and fuss with each other at personality levels, but most usually manage to quickly adjust and overcome such petty behaviors.

Time is always on our side. The soul which connects soul mates stands persistently *centered* and immutably balanced *behind* all earth-shaking outer events. Problems come and go, but what can divide that which is always serenely and securely there? Are there break-ups or separations? Yes, and mostly from ignorance and that variety of "X" factors within and between all relationships. Though soul mates meet at a point of equalization at the soul level, they are rarely exactly at equal degrees of development. One may also be polarized mentally, while the other deals predominantly with emotions. Even if they are close in their degree of spiritual communion, there may be a wide communication gap at personality or other levels between them that needs to be bridged.

Soul mates are soul mates because they have a communication level between them *at a soul level.* At that level, there is no problem. There, they see eye to eye. Nevertheless, this leaves the wide range of daily life lived by both of them at personality, mental, emotional, and physical levels. Any one of these levels may be seeded with temporary disturbances, needed to be recognized and overcome. Divorce, or even a temporary separation is quite unusual between soul mates, even in our extremely decadent "modern" civilization. It would take a great amount of upset or imbalance at the personality or lesser three levels to destroy the poised soul relationship within.

Soul mates are normal individuals like you and me who are at-one with the soul partner in life. They experience all the normal trials, joys, sorrows, and the plethora of dramatic impacts engaged here and there along the highways and byways of life. I found and I live with my soul mate. I can report first hand that we encounter crisis after crisis between ourselves and outer-life circumstances on a regular basis. These challenges have helped both of us to grow immensely. We have a heaven on Earth marriage! We both know and appreciate that Earth provides us with the opportunities to enjoy the ecstasy of loving communion while we experiment, experience, and express sacred life. May this same ecstasy be yours soon.

May the heavens open and pour down a great divine flow of Light, Love, and Power into your life, into the lives of your loved ones, and into your work. So be it!

14

Soul-Mating:
A Rapidly Growing Phenomenon

The everturning wheel of time unfolds a bright new vista. The one stands tall on the horizon.

At this time, we come to a more truly scientific definition of soul mates. It is not the "meeting-at-the-soul-level" definition that we have related to up to this point. It transcends it. Prepare yourself for a quantum leap in your comprehension. The term "twin-soul" now comes closer to a real soul mate definition, but it is still inadequate. You are half of a pair, meaning if you are a female, there is a male counterpart of you. This equally balanced polarity division is universal in scope. All forms of life come in opposed electrical pairs, from the smallest speck of dust to the hottest blazing suns.

Normally, it is rare for an entity to link up physically with their exact counterpart, male or female. It happens with ever increasing frequency during a major planetary change, like the one occurring now on Earth. This present civilization is about to move out of The Age of Slaughter into The Age of Character. For only as character is known and developed can a quantum leap in light consciousness, or knowing, occur. True marriage relationships are about to begin, and an equal and balanced interchange between mates will become normal. They are abnormal, or quite rare, now.

Twin-soul relationships and soul mate relationships are very different. Soul mate relationships are beginning to be frequent or common, but twin-soul alignments are still few and far between. Thankfully, this is about to change and hopefully, you, yourself, will play a strong lead in the change.

There is only one truth, not many. God alone is truth. There are as many different perceptions of truth as there are minds. Not one of these different perceptions can phase or alter the one truth, for it is law. The truth is that God has established immutable laws that no person can alter. The same law that governs the Magnetic Universe governs the Electric Universe. These primary laws of God and Creation have been known and used by the ancient illumined masters and adepts on Earth, and by the Pleiadian civilization many thousands of years ago.

At the phenomenal or electrical beginning, the ONE divided and multiplied into the MANY *lights*. Each one of these fragmented parts, or divided lights, is half of an exact duplicate of the One Whole Light. All pairs of us must then return to the ONE, our source. Each one of us is half of a pair wanting to be fused back into the ONENESS of God. The inner God is whole and undivided always!

While in manifestation, each separate God part is distinctly polarized as a female or male form. Without it, duality, or the commencement of dimension, would not be possible. Though each half unit is distinctly male or female, each has its own law of oneness. This is because the ONE is centered within every form of life without exception. Thus in all kingdoms of nature the masculine and feminine units are constantly striving to unite and find balance with an equal mate. This same law of action applies in the mineral kingdom, as well. Atoms, bees, humans, whatever, all exist with singular polarized male or female identities and bodies to match. Each relates to another in its own species or field of existence. Night is the charging or male part of a single day wave-cycle. Day is the discharging, female half of the cycle. Compression is masculine; expansion is feminine. Space is male; mass is female. The cube is female; the circle is male. All forms, fields, and dimensions are governed by this immutable law of balance.

In subhuman kingdoms, an aware interaction between polarized units of one happens only at physical levels. Emotional lures—

like sweet tones, brilliant colors, erotic perfumes and other such—are used to attract counterparts, climaxing in a sexual union.

In our aware human kingdom, we use all four levels of impression or impact—physical, emotional, mental, and intuitive (or soul)—as contact points sexually between female and male. Thus, we are greatly enriched in our capacity to merge and blend at several equal levels.

Twin-souls are perfect mirrors or reflections of each other. Other terms like twin-flames, astrological twins, kindred spirits, simply add a maze of confusion. It is easy to observe that often well-meaning but ignorant individuals have imposed their own limited beliefs on various life sciences, thus misconstruing the meaning. Many of the most important biblical truths have been intentionally deleted or changed to further the control of various rulers and priests. The universally known doctrine of rebirth, or reincarnation, was deliberately removed from the Bible. At other times, the "adversarial forces of darkness," all those against God awareness have utilized agents in church and government to confuse and delude the masses, thus hoping to delay the present work of "the light forces." They will fail, for true love, marriage, soul mates and the One God concepts are eternally woven in the tapestry of the heavens and earths for all to see. God always wins!

The time of soul-mating is now. In this golden new Age of Character, the conscious urge of soul mates to yearn for, search, and couple with their balanced counterparts grows daily. Where, oh where, is she or he, this brilliant star rising in our future heavens? In the distant night of time, there may have been a special someone who is back again, waiting and wanting your presence. We are in a tumultuous age, when all things assume extreme proportions, the old rapidly crumbles and the new arises out of the ashes. For a while the huge differences between these ages is overly pronounced. Soon the familiar old energy fades and the strange new energy becomes familiar to public consciousness. In this awakening Age of Character, His Holy Presence awakens within the vanguard of the masses and brings a grand reunion with our polar mate.

Our twin-soul may or may not be physically incarnate at the same time as we are. In that case, there may or may not be a possibility of reunion. If you will remember you are not your physical body nor this personality known to you in this brief one lifetime, your understanding will come. Your eternal connection with your twin-soul is beyond space and time. Time itself is a grand illusion.

Time is not what it appears to be. To our soul and spirit, time, as understood in earthly measurements, does not exist. The illusion that events are separated into this day and that day, or this lifetime and that lifetime, occurs only in the brain. At a soul and spirit level, all time is One. Division of the great Eternal Now does not exist. Therefore, we are always at a state of union or oneness with our twin-soul in the realm of soul or self.

The Age of Character is here. Twin-souls and soul mates are moving one by one into alignment with each other. Male and female are enjoying the sacred ecstasy of the holy (whole-I) soul and spirit permeating the core of being. Until this balanced dual union happens, single life continues to be a persistent, restless yearning, a deep longing to find at-one-ment or fusion with our mind's and heart's desire.

In reality, twin-souls are never really divided. God is undivided. Only at form levels do divisions appear to exist. As every cell of the body divides and reproduces billions of cells, each following the exact pattern set within it, so God divided the God-Self.

To know self is to know God-Self. It is important, if we are soul-mating, to know ourselves. The "know thyself" adage attributed to the Greeks goes much further back into antiquity. The Greeks merely rephrased the great underlying truth: until we know our own quality and substance, it is impossible to really know the quality and substance in others, and specifically in our twin soul.

Through millions of years of evolution we are now aware of "other selves" because we first became aware of self. Once self-awareness was established, the next extended awareness of duality—or self and mirror other-than-self, or soul mate—became possible. Duality permits two-dimensional perspectives. Three-dimensional reality issued from the three-fold division of the ONE. The two God-Selves could only emerge from the one God that had preceded and extended them into time, space, and motion, or a three-dimensional field. Thus began the primary Trinity. A Triune God-

Head was established. Does it matter if this Trinity is called, Father, Son and Holy Spirit or Shiva, Vishnu and Brahma? Not one iota! The followers of both these major religions are naming and defining their own unique approach to this primary Trinity of Creation. The Law of Three relates to the Undivided One, standing behind and extending the Divided Two into a many dimensioned form (or cosmos).

A dream thought, or dream experience is true at a dream level. Approached from a wide-awake physical consciousness within your personality, it appears not true. You know it is only a dream, and has, therefore, no reality or truth in our three-dimensional plane. On the other hand, from the viewpoint of your dreaming self, looking back toward your outer-plane physical consciousness view, what you and I think of as our *real life* is to your dreaming self, the "dream" that our inner self (or inner consciousness, our soul), is dreaming! Which viewpoint is right, or true? Both! Each one is true at its level of existence.

You are one being, yet you are also spirit, soul, and body, exemplifying the Law of Three. Each one is true at its level. Carrying this thought another big leap, you also consist of seven basic layers of electricity, or seven coats of skin, as phrased in the Book of Genesis. These names will vary in the different schools of thought, but the essence is the same:

1) Physical body

2) Emotional body

3) Mental body

4) Soul, or intuitive body

5) God, The Whole I Am Spirit Body

6) God, The Divided/Multiplied Mother/Father Body

7) GOD, THE UNDIVIDED BODY AND SPIRIT

As you know, the average person remains identified or focused in the first three bodies listed. He or she is just now beginning to be aware of the soul or intuitive essence. If he or she taps into this essence, he or she stands out among all humankind.

Just think about the splendid order of all creation. There are no accidents within it. Every speck, shape, and level of life is in the right place, at the right time, with the right male or female motion. The biology, geometry, and mathematics of the universe are exact and true. Knowing these laws, if only minutely for now, gives us great confidence in our lives, in our own being, in the stability and eternalness of the world, and in the One Great Life we term God, within and behind it and centered in ourselves.

No true teacher ever gives false information intentionally. I have presented what I know and think about all of these matters. I hope it will stimulate you to know and think for yourself. I earnestly hope you will soon find that twin-soul who is sounding your note at this very instant. He or she is calling. Listen and you shall hear!

May the dove of peace descend into the depth of your being. May you be another bright station of light within the ascending arc of Christ in you. May a golden strand of consciousness link you with your own attractive, reflective and beloved twin-soul soon! So be it.

15

Sex in the Cosmos

The sublime chase never ends
The two are one.
All are wed under cosmic
moon and sun.

Sex is everything in many more ways than one. Without sex, soul mates could not exist and you would not be here this day reading this sentence. That is very primary. Sex goes far beyond "jumping in the sack" or "making love." The entire body of this universe is sexual. The smallest particle of mass within it is sexual.

Why? I was hoping you would ask!

When THE UNDIVIDED GOD of still magnetic light began creating the divided and multiplied universe of electricity and seeming reality, that division brought forth the father/mother/male/female polarity. That gift of love would forever be re-given to subsequent and continuous creating. The energy given to the father simultaneously was given back to the mother; thus began the pulse or heartbeat of the universe, of all the cosmos which multiplied and divided thereafter. Thus, soul mates are created.

That sexual interchange must go on endlessly between all divided and multiplied units of the Electric Universe. Compression and expansion, the pump or piston of the largest star to the smallest

particle in an atom are simply male/female interactions. Compression produces hot dryness and expansion produces wet coldness. These are the only two basic substances in the creating cycle. Only two basic geometrical forms are the basis for all other forms in the cosmos, the cold cube of space and the hot sphere generated from compression. In turn, the hot sphere or sun cools through expansion, to once again form a cold cube. This compression/expansion cycle goes on *ad infinitum*.

I also want to mention here that this inbreathing/outbreathing, or folding/unfolding, takes place in the tiniest particle and has at one point—when the electric wave is at amplitude (at high or low point of trough)—a most tiny, but real, sun, as real as our own young sun in the heavens above Earth.

Sex has been greatly abused and misused on our earth. It's about time this sex principle is understood to uplift and benefit people rather than control and debase them. No matter what aspect of duality—up/down, in/out, hard/soft, cold/warm, wet/dry—the male/female polarity is equally divided in them. The hot suns or incandescent spheres are male, while the cold cube of space is female. Compression is male; expansion is female; centripetal motion is male; centrifugal motion is female. Everything from whatever viewpoint—chemical, electrical, optical, the light spectrum and even octaves of sound—can be identified from the male/female sex principle within and behind it. The entire periodic table of elements is now mostly known, and any metal can now be melted or cooled to become transmuted into another element. Every atom of existence is composed of an electrical light wave. There is no exterior difference between the atoms in a butterfly, or a human being, or a cloud in the sky. The identity of any form is recorded and retained forever in the nine inert gases, within the nine complete octaves of the periodic table of elements.

In our upcoming Age of Character, sex will be known as more than a little three-letter word. The full understanding of sex as the basis of all the kingdoms of nature will bring civilization to a 1,000-year advance in ten years. The complete data is discussed in *The Pleiadian Documents*, mentioned earlier. As ten enlightened souls tell ten more enlightened souls, who go on telling ten more, *ad infinitum*, the entire population of Earth will literally light up. I hope you will discover these truths and pass them along to ten ready awakening souls you know. Meanwhile, I am sure you are going to be delighted as your own true sex education begins.

16

The Science of True Mates

Not one by one, but two by two, enter you into the gate of my new kingdom.

All relationships can be enduring providing that a balanced interchange occurs between all "relations" involved. In the new science here now on earth, the key word of that science is balance. The second word to help fill out the idea more fully is rhythmic. The final word, bringing the entire continuous process of creating together locally and universally is interchange. Put them together and we have rhythmic balanced interchange.

Study each one of these words carefully and see how they blend together perfectly. The entire story of creating is contained within them. The balanced folding/unfolding mates forever seek to unite with the oneness. This cannot be done in the Electric Universe, only in the Magnetic Universe. Therefore the pendulum keeps swinging nonstop. Male and female give equally to each other, unite, or rest only for a moment, to repeat the process again without end.

In your very real, down-to-earth life your equal will come into your physical experience when you want it strongly enough. Then, whether or not that interchange goes on and on with that person depends entirely on equal giving and re-giving between the two of you. If one partner in the union is a *taker,* then the union will soon dissolve, no matter how glamorous or attractive it looks on the surface. Nature always sets the greatest example of wisdom around us. Nature never takes, it only gives. Only the human, acting as an equal co-creator with God, takes and destroys himself and nature along with it. The law of love never changes—simply give what you have been given and abundance overflows everywhere! Take a good look at your own life habits; are you a taker or giver? Be honest in your appraisal, for you fool no one but yourself, and anyone who does that is the greatest fool of all!

Have there been times—perhaps even moments—this day when you could have re-given what you hold so abundantly? When everyone involved in exchanges receives their balanced share, harmony presides. The opposite occurs when anyone is "shorted," even if nothing is said or done about it at that moment.

Your equal and yourself have been drawn together because you balance each other out. You are also wonderful reflectors or mirrors of each other. Growth of a personal nature can now be accelerated immensely. What is important is not what you can get out of a relationship, it is what you can give to it. If there is an obvious imbalance between you and your mate, look to see what *you* can do about it first. When you point a finger at your twin-soul you are pointing it at yourself! The time for "victim consciousness" belongs to the old ages. This is the beginning of the Age of Character. No one else did it to you. Your reality is entirely self-made. If you do not like it, change it. Usually a simple change of attitude works miracles!

A true mate, in summary, is the other half of what you are. When you give your all to your mate, you will be re-given all. Your life will be joyously fulfilled. You earned it yourself!

Dr. Michael is the author of ten self-improvement books. He is a former professional basketball player, published songwriter, television host of his own series, *The Mysteries of Life*, and has taught psychology at the University of Humanistic Studies in San Diego, California. In 1984, he was awarded the distinguished Bronze Halo Award by The Southern California Motion Picture Council, for his contribution as an author, lecturer, philanthropist, and humanitarian.